The Collaborative Classroom

A guide to co-operative learning

Susan Hill & Tim Hill

Heinemann
Portsmouth, New Hampshire

To David Johnson and Roger Johnson whose ideas inspired this book.

Heinemann Educational Books, Inc.
361 Hanover Street   Portsmouth, NH 03801-3959
Offices and agents throughout the world

Copyright © 1990 by Susan Hill & Tim Hill

Library of Congress-Cataloging-in-Publication Data
Hill, Susan.
   The collaborative classroom: a guide to co-operative
   learning
   Susan Hill & Timothy Hill.
   p.   cm.
   Includes Bibliographical references.
   ISBN 0-435-08525-5
   I. Team learning approach in education. I. Hill, Timothy
   II. Title.
   LB10S2.H48   1990
   371.3'95-dc20
   89-77378   CIP

Published simultaneously in 1990
in the United States by Heinemann
and in Australia by
Eleanor Curtain Publishing
2 Hazeldon Place
South Yarra 3141

Reprinted in the United States 1991
by Edwards Brothers, Inc.

Production by Sylvana Scannapiego,
Island Graphics
Designed by Sarn Potter
Illustrations by Kate Edwards
Cover design by David Constable
Cover illustration by Veronica Oborn
Typeset in 12/14 Baskerville and Futura
by Trade Graphics Pty Ltd

FOREWORD

◆

This book is about people learning and working together, rather than alone. It is a timely and important publication. As teachers, we are recognising the power of, and need for, co-operation. We now know that children learn more effectively when they work together, that they build healthier relationships with themselves and others this way, and that the future survival of our planet will be determined by the way in which people and nations co-operate. It is also timely in the sense that we are faced with increasing challenges and demands in our profession. The craft of teaching is too complex for a lone journey — we need support. When we build co-operative partnerships and share the journey with others, we become part of a supportive team where ownership and responsibility are shared and we are all empowered.

The Collaborative Classroom is an exciting addition to the co-operative learning literature. Sue and Tim not only help us to understand what co-operation means and why it is important, but they also make explicit a range of practical processes and strategies that help to build and maintain a truly co-operative classroom. Moreover, they are ideas that have been developed in conjunction with practising teachers — they work!

Use this book as a valuable resource — talk about the ideas with your colleagues, try them out, and further develop and share your own.

Joan Dalton

CONTENTS

◆

PREFACE

Back in 1986, during a hot Christmas holiday, we sat on a beach talking about how our work had many overlapping themes. Sue's interests lay in communication, literacy and literature; Tim had been working in the area of social competency and children's friendships.

Co-operative learning, which relies so much on spoken and written language, was the obvious meeting place for our interests. Whether we would still be together and co-operating after working on a book about co-operation was a risk we decided to take. Time went by and we sat around and talked about ways children can work co-operatively. But it was Betty Fox, principal of a small Catholic school, who stirred us into action. She invited us to talk with teachers at her school.

The school, St Bernadette's, has 120 students. One-third of the students come from low income families. Another third come from more affluent homes. The remaining students come from nearby middle class areas. There are fifteen different ethnic backgrounds represented at the school and most of these families do not speak English at home. The school accepts children with special needs and has a special education mainstreaming policy. Some children are referred to the school by the sisters of St Joseph who run a family care unit. Most people see the school as small and compassionate.

Talking with the teachers led us to write this book. We wanted to record all the good ideas that were generated by working with children and talking together at staff meetings and conferences during 1988. The teachers — Betty Fox, Cathy Sibenaler, Ros Ellis, Anne Weygood, Dianne Bidmeade, Karen Zuvich and Paul Hollis — read and critiqued the many drafts.

Later, in 1989, the teachers at Taperoo Primary School helped us refine many of the ideas. We soon found that co-operative learning has limitless possibilities for all curriculum areas. The principal, Polly Eckert, and teachers Anna Wienert, Barb Hodgins, Sue Ryan, Greg Adams and Lyn Thompson also provided rich insights into the benefits of co-operative learning for students in disadvantaged schools.

David Prideaux at the South Australian College of Advanced Education, Magill read and provided critical feedback on the manuscript. Several other readers helped us with suggestions for ideas: Joelie Hancock, Tom Swift, Rosemary Sandstrom, Chris Hastwell, Merry Scotney-Turbill and Jane O'Loughlin and her Year 6 class. Two students studying at Magill, Alice Berry and Helen Steele, also provided feedback. Ray Stradwick took the photographs. Thank you all.

1

INTRODUCTION

We sink or swim together.
— Johnson & Johnson

We are all familiar with individualised learning. There are times when we want to do something on our own: research a topic that interests us, read a book, or perhaps write a story. There are also times when we might be challenged through competition, such as playing in our local netball team.

As teachers, we can plan individualised programs in the classroom so that every child works as a lonely long-distance runner. We can also plan learning experiences and set up our classrooms competitively so that children perform like racing car drivers, striving constantly for the winning post. Or we can plan co-operative programs where children learn to work together, as valued and mutually dependent team members.

Individualised and competitive learning situations are common in children's school experiences; co-operative learning is less so. But research shows that co-operative learning has significant advantages, for both intellectual and social development, over individualised and competitive learning environments.

BENEFITS OF COLLABORATIVE LEARNING

HIGHER ACHIEVEMENT

Piagetian and behaviourist approaches view the intellect as a characteristic of the individual. More recent theories place much greater emphasis on the social development of the intellect. Rather than viewing intelligence as an individual's property, it is seen as a process where individuals construct and organise their actions together upon the environment. Doise and Mugny (1984) have conducted research which supports their contentions that social interaction does lead to more advanced cognitive development.

Johnson and Johnson's research also provides overwhelming evidence that co-operative learning experiences promote higher academic achievements than do individualistic or competitive learning experiences. They have conducted twenty-six classroom studies that involved achievement data for primary and secondary students of varying abilities and ages, and in a wide variety of curriculum areas. There was evidence of significantly higher achievement in twenty-one of the twenty-six studies. Of the remaining five, two had mixed results and three found no difference.

Johnson, Maruyama, Johnson, Nelson and Skon (1981) conducted a meta-analysis of the 122 studies that had been conducted in this area between 1924 and 1981. Co-operative learning experiences promoted higher achievements than did individualised or competitive learning experiences. They found that students working within a co-operative situation achieved at about the 80th percentile of those working within a competitive or individualistic situation.

Recent theory, experimental evidence and studies conducted in class-rooms all suggest that if schools are to provide for the optimum intellectual development of their students, relationships amongst children and the kinds of co-operative activities children engage in will need to be taken seriously. Teaching the skills of collaborative learning, group management and organisation will become more important than instruction and imparting knowledge.

DEEPER UNDERSTANDING

Collaborative learning works for young children in pre-schools as readily as for a team of lawyers working on a difficult legal brief. It is often the case that we can toss ideas around for longer and are more motivated to continue learning when we work together. Hearing different points of view, the clash of minds, the 'exchange' of ideas, the listing of problems and their solutions, all contribute to the development of thinking skills and deeper levels of understanding.

LEARNING IS ENJOYABLE

Children and adults alike learn more and achieve more and actually have more fun in co-operative learning groups. Our personal experiences certainly back this up. We often became frustrated with the views of other people we worked with when they challenged us, but this stirred us to reassess positions we had previously held firmly. Most importantly we realised that in working together and playing with ideas we were enjoying ourselves. (It is also true that we had to call on all our co-operative social skills at times to keep the pair or group functioning and afloat.)

DEVELOPING LEADERSHIP SKILLS

Collaborative learning provides continual opportunities for the development of important leadership and group skills. Children with these learning experiences are more able to understand another's perspective and have better developed interaction skills than do those from competitive or individualistic settings (Johnson & Johnson 1983, 1987).

PROMOTING POSITIVE ATTITUDES

Research shows that when the environment is structured to allow them to work together co-operatively, children are more positive about school, subject areas and their teachers. Furthermore, regardless of differences in ability or ethnic background, children are more positive about each other after working together co-operatively than after working within

competitive or individualistic learning structures. Co-operative learning environments also encourage more positive expectations about working with others and taking part in resolving differences (Cooper et al 1980; Johnson & Johnson 1981, 1983, 1987).

PROMOTING SELF-ESTEEM

There is evidence that compared with alternative learning structures, co-operative learning environments promote higher levels of self-esteem in children. Norem-Hebeison and Johnson (1981) also found that co-operative learning experiences promote healthier processes for deriving conclusions about one's self-worth, and that attitudes towards co-operation tended to be related to self-acceptance and positive self-evaluation. Competitiveness, on the other hand, tended to be related to conditional self-acceptance (you have to keep winning to accept yourself), and a positive attitude towards individualistic situations tended to be related to self-rejection.

INCLUSIVE LEARNING

Learning together, including others in co-operative learning groups and setting up a collaborative classroom environment actively promote care and respect for others. Positive peer relationships are built, ways to communicate ideas develop, and most importantly, the perspectives of others are more easily understood.

Inclusive co-operative learning is especially important when children in the classroom come from different backgrounds and have a wide range of abilities. The successful mainstreaming of exceptional children into regular classes requires a collaborative effort. Special children can play a valuable role in the classroom but only where the class works actively to accept and include them.

Co-operative learning also has important implications in the development of mutual respect and better understanding between girls and boys. Learning to work together, sharing group roles and solving problems in a co-operative way promote the self-esteem of everyone because all the children and their teachers have an important and valued role to play.

A SENSE OF BELONGING

There are some children whose prior socialisation means that they may not be well suited to achievement in traditional learning environments. When these children make little academic progress their motivation to learn and self-esteem suffer. They become caught in a self-defeating cycle: in order to satisfy their own needs for recognition and belonging they become disruptive and are then classed as a behaviour problem. Alternatively, they withdraw and give up.

A collaborative learning environment has enormous potential for these children. It satisfies for their needs for recognition and belonging through their involvement in worthwhile activities.

SKILLS FOR THE FUTURE

The co-operative skills necessary to work effectively in a group are essential not only for learning in schools but also for success in the workplace and getting on with people at home.

◆

2

COLLABORATING

TO LEARN

Union gives strength.

———————————————————◆———————————————————

Collaborative classrooms operate on three important principles:
1. Co-operative skills are taught, practised and feedback is given on how well the skills were used.
2. The class is encouraged to operate as a cohesive group.
3. Individuals are given responsibility for their own learning and behaviour.
  Strategies related to these three principles are not mutually exclusive but operate in a cyclical way, i.e. the promotion of co-operative skills will also promote cohesiveness and responsibility.

WHAT IS CO-OPERATION?

Before examining each of these principles in detail, we need to establish what is meant by the term 'co-operation'.

Co-operation is often used in relation to children's compliance with authority. We might say, 'We are co-operating well, aren't we?' when everyone is sitting still and quietly in a group. Co-operation is also used when referring to children with 'nice manners' who share their materials or move out of people's way. These might be appropriate social behaviours in certain circumstances but they do not mean that children are necessarily taking part in a co-operative learning activity. Co-operative learning is not about harmonising. It often involves intellectual conflict.

A co-operative activity can be said to exist when two or more people are working together towards the same goal. *The two essential elements in any co-operative activity are goal similarity and positive interdependence.*

GOAL SIMILARITY

The more similar the goals of the children in the group, the more co-operative the activity is likely to be. At times children may appear to be working co-operatively when asking for the spelling of a word or sharing pencils while drawing but they may well have their own separate goals in these cases.

To work co-operatively the children's goals need not be exactly coincidental but they must be similar. If a class is working together on a play, the group goal is to produce a play which other children in the school will enjoy and appreciate. Each child's goal may not be exactly the same: one child may be wanting to please the teacher, another wants the attention of classmates and others really want an opportunity to work the lights. But the more similar the goals the more co-operative the activity.

POSITIVE INTERDEPENDENCE

The second essential element for any activity to be truly co-operative is positive interdependence — the view held by group members that they can only succeed if they work together.

Positive interdependence between individuals can be fostered in a number of ways:

- Give group members specific roles to perform such as 'encourager', 'observer', 'clarifier', or 'recorder'. (See pages 45–59 for details.) In this way each individual has a specific task to perform and everybody's contribution is necessary to complete the task successfully.
- Break the task into subtasks which are necessary to complete the task successfully. Each group member is given a subtask. Input is then required by all members of the group.
- Assess the group as one entity instead of individually. Children could be asked to work on their spelling in pairs, for example, with an assessment of each pair.
- Co-operative and competitive goal structures can be combined (see Slavin et al 1985) by having co-operative learning groups compete against each other. (Sporting teams competing is an example of this strategy.) This competition engenders positive interdependence within the co-operative group, but it is essential that group members are changed frequently to avoid fostering competing cliques that can undermine class cohesiveness and morale.
- Pit a small group against some external force, such as time or gravity. Two children could, for example, see how long they can keep a ball suspended using only their foreheads. Competing against an external force is very different from competing against each other.
- Create fantasy situations where the group has to work together to deal with imaginary forces, within rules established by the situation, e.g. 'You are on an island and must create a house, farms and a self-sufficient community.'

Putting on a group or class play, publishing a co-operative newspaper or setting up a doctor's surgery for dramatic play in pre-school all provide for similar goals and positive interdependence. In these examples, group members have important roles to play so that the group can function co-operatively. All roles are interdependent and individual children share similar goals such as performing for an audience, informing others with a newspaper or making sure the doctor's surgery has a good supply of patients as well as doctors and nurses.

LEARNING CO-OPERATIVE SKILLS

Co-operative skills are not inherited, nor do they appear magically. Social skills are learned. Give children opportunities to observe and practise co-operative skills and, with the appropriate encouragement, they will learn them. In every classroom there are some children who have had fewer opportunities to learn and practise the skills than other children, but the process of teaching the skills is the same for all: *make the skill explicit, provide practice, and give feedback and encourage reflection.*

In the collaborative classroom the teacher and children are continually engaged in the process of observing, practising and giving feedback about the effectiveness of their co-operative skills.

WHAT ARE CO-OPERATIVE SKILLS?

There are four broad areas where co-operative skills are needed: forming groups, working as a group, problem solving as a group and managing differences (based in part on Johnson and Johnson 1986). The co-operative skills overlap and there are times, for example, when those children engaged in problem solving suddenly need to revive the skills for listening.

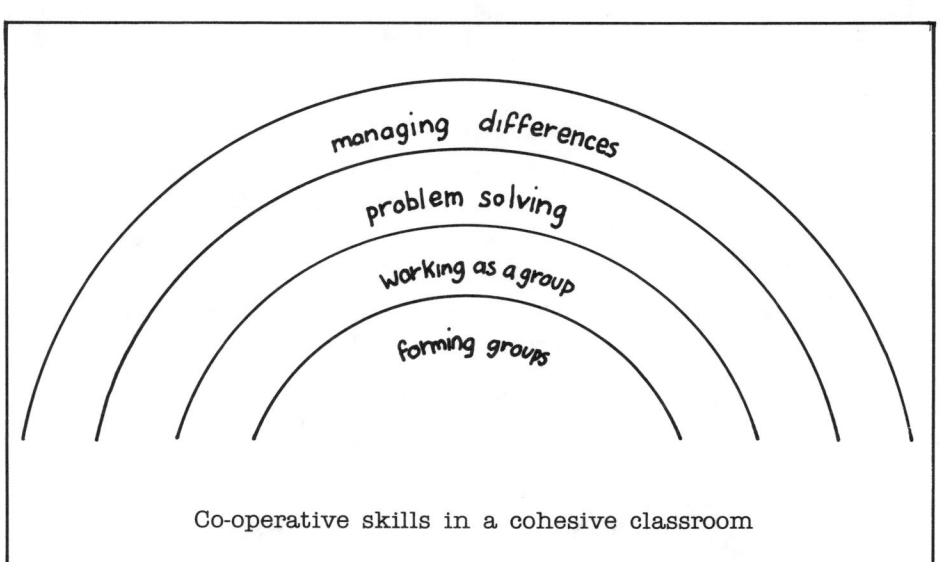

managing differences

problem solving

working as a group

forming groups

Co-operative skills in a cohesive classroom

FORMING GROUPS

Whenever we form pairs or groups, co-operative skills are needed. This is most apparent when we are asked to work with others we do not know or those we see as different. In general children find it easier working in groups with close friends, but other configurations should also be used.

There are several advantages to heterogeneous groups where children with specialised co-operative skills can act as models for children who will benefit by seeing these skills in action. In mixed groups children have opportunities to learn more about children of different gender and from different cultural and ability groups. Some of the skills children may need to start working as a group include:

- making space for people
- making pairs or circles
- making eye contact
- staying with the group
- using quiet voices
- using people's names
- eliminating put-downs

- taking turns
- keeping hands and feet to themselves
- forming groups without bothering others
- allowing one person to speak
- active listening

(Children can be encouraged to suggest additions to this list.)

WORKING AS A GROUP

Having formed a group or pair there are many ways to ensure that it works effectively. Assigning roles — some people know them as leadership roles — is a great way to structure a group so that it is positively interdependent.

While traditionally we have assigned a leader or a chairperson to lead a group there are many advantages in sharing the task of leadership. Each of the following roles encourages the use of those leadership skills that make up the co-operative skills necessary for working as a group:

- observer
- recorder
- questioner
- summariser
- encourager
- clarifier
- organiser
- time-keeper etc.

PROBLEM SOLVING AS A GROUP

To solve problems as a group children can develop skills that include the following:

- defining the problem
- brainstorming
- clarifying ideas
- confirming ideas
- elaborating ideas
- seeing consequences
- criticising ideas
- organising information
- finding solutions

MANAGING DIFFERENCES

The skills required for managing differences are important both at school and for the future. Looking at problems from a different perspective, learning to negotiate and mediate when the conflict gets 'hot' are skills that not only make life and learning in school more co-operative but also overlap and influence ways children relate to others at home. The skills for managing differences are:

- stating positions
- seeing the problem from another viewpoint
- negotiating
- mediating
- reaching consensus

The development of co-operative skills is at the core of the collaborative classroom. However, the feeling of belonging or cohesion within a classroom promotes the disposition to be co-operative.

COHESIVENESS IN THE CLASSROOM

The existing social groupings within any class are often accepted as a permanent reality. Boys choose to work with boys, girls work with other girls, the very articulate sit with other talkers and the quiet, withdrawn children sit alone. But in a cohesive class everyone sees himself or herself as belonging to one group that they value more highly than any subgroup and a social hierarchy is not obvious or well defined.

Cohesiveness is essential for effective collaboration. It is related to children's motivation to be co-operative, to accept others, to learn from others and to be empathetic. The success of a teacher will depend to a large extent on whether the class is united and working towards some common purpose. Failure to create a cohesive classroom will affect how children learn, both intellectually and socially.

To create cohesiveness we need to look at the way we inadvertently reinforce existing social structures. Understanding the factors that lead to divisiveness in the classroom can be promoted by open discussion, by talking about the values, attitudes and behaviours associated with people's gender, race, ethnic group or physical appearance. Children need to confront taken-for-granted beliefs and the way in which these beliefs affect our lives. All the class members will need to work actively to break down the sociological barriers to cohesiveness that exist in any classroom.

There are many ways in which we can actively intervene to promote cohesiveness:

1. Open discussions that promote understanding of sociological factors that create barriers to cohesiveness.
2. Regularly change the membership of small co-operative groups.
3. Promote the establishment of groups that are heterogeneous with regard to gender, ability and cultural background.
4. Establish activities in which the whole class is involved and where everyone has a role to play, e.g. class newspapers, plays, murals, whole class discussions like class meetings (see pages 86–95).
5. Play co-operative games and co-operative sports activities.

6. Participate in activities that aim to build trust between individuals in the class.

COHESIVENESS AND TRUST

Cohesive classrooms are based on trust, the risk of sharing personal opinions and feelings with another who may either support those ideas or put them down and ridicule the discloser. Trust builds when people openly share personal opinions and information, when encouragement is given, and when verbal and non-verbal put-downs are eliminated. Once children know that a teacher and other children can be trusted not to ridicule, and will also share or disclose personal opinions, more risks in expressing new ideas and feelings will be taken.

The following suggestions for activities can help build trusting relationships and a cohesive class:

- Identify and list verbal and non-verbal 'put-downs'.
- Identify and list verbal and non-verbal 'build-ups'.
- Role play how to handle 'put-downs'.
- Role play how to handle family and classroom conflicts.
- Use a buddy system where students draw a classmate's name from a hat and do kind things for that person. (They do not reveal their identity.)

- Make large murals of all the children's faces and the faces of the teachers. This shows that all are members of a group.
- Make a classroom banner or quilt from small squares of material illustrated by all the class members. Hobbytex or embroidery can be used to illustrate the squares. The squares can be made to be children's faces or hobbies.

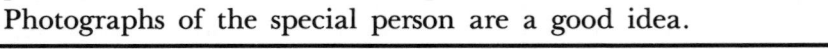

- Children write examples of co-operative behaviour on coloured circles, which are then glued to make a collage.
- Trace around the body or draw a hand of each member of the class. Write words to describe the positive features of the person on the cut-out shape.
- Have a special person of the week. Take turns to have one special person each week. Children write positive comments about that person. Photographs of the special person are a good idea.

- Trace around hands. Each person writes: 'I'm handy to have around because . . .'
- Give feedback on positive encouraging behaviours demonstrated by people in the group.
- Ask the children to list the things they do to co-operate, and write their suggestions on a wheel. To practise the skills a spinner can be turned and where it stops the children role play or explain where or when this skill is practised. Alternatively turn the spinner at the beginning of the day or recess time and each person takes one skill to practise.

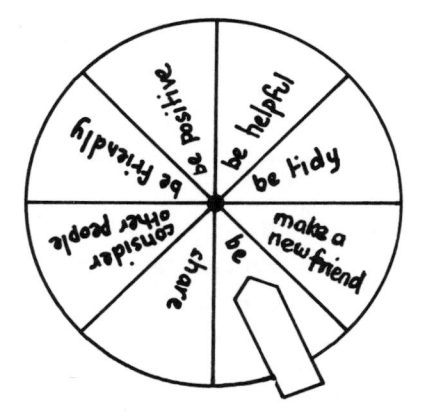

- In pairs children cut out shapes. These can be decorated and positive words or good things to say about partners are written on each shape.
- Create a 'positive sandwich' by asking a child to say something positive immediately before and after making a negative statement. In this way the criticism is 'sandwiched' between positive feedback.
- Children can keep lists of 'What I can do' in language, mathematics, and other areas of the curriculum. Some teachers keep 'What I can do' books where children describe what they can do in more detail. Pages can be added to the book as the year progresses.

What I can do ...

I can write sentences
I can write research
I can use a dictionary
I can learn my words
I can write letters
I can read

I'am glad I'm me because I am friendly ...

- Circle time can be a time for sharing positive thoughts. Start off round the circle saying:

    Child 1: 'I'm glad I'm me because...'
    Child 2: 'You're glad you're you because you...'

This can be repeated around the circle. Children only repeat the sentence from their near neighbour. This helps children think of others' strengths as well as their own.

- Have a co-operation box in the classroom. It could be like a postbox made out of a carton or an old decorated shoebox. When children

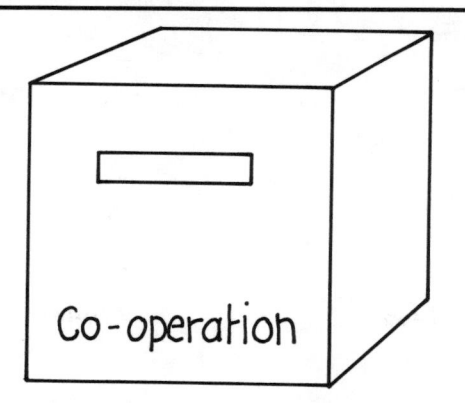

Co-operation

have co-operated well they can draw a picture and write about what they did and post it. On Friday the letters can be read. Another way to do this is to remind the children of co-operative skills such as taking turns, using quiet voices, looking at the speaker, making encouraging comments or saying friendly things. They then take a piece of paper and write or draw a picture of someone in the class who co-operated or was friendly during the week. The comments and drawings could then be discussed.

TAKING RESPONSIBILITY

Children are motivated to learn and behave appropriately when they are encouraged to take responsibility for themselves (Glasser 1986). Responsibility can be developed by providing a democratic style of leadership that includes:

1. Providing clear guidelines for the teacher's role and responsibility.
2. Providing clear guidelines for the students' roles and their responsibilities.
3. Involving children in negotiation and decision making about curriculum content, classroom rules and consequences, timetables etc.

4. Encouraging children to take responsibility for their own actions.
5. Providing opportunities for students to monitor and evaluate their own learning.
6. Providing opportunities for students to evaluate their own behaviour.
7. Providing lots of open-ended activities with a wide range of student choice.
8. Encouraging students' negotiating and decision-making skills.

THE TEACHER'S ROLE

Teaching becomes an impossible job when we take on the responsibility for making all children behave in certain ways, the responsibility for making children learn exactly what they are told and the responsibility for solving all the social problems that exist in the class. This kind of teacher 'over-responsibility' is not in the best interests of the children or teachers.

'Over-responsible' teachers encourage children to be dependent and reduce children's internal motivation to learn. Furthermore when we are over-responsible, children are inadvertently encouraged to interfere with

planned classroom activities because it is the only way they can meet their own needs for power, fun and belonging (Glasser 1986).

Children can be encouraged to take responsibility for their own learning and behaviour. Too often children come to see school as a place that organises them, where things are done for them and not as a place where they learn to do things for themselves. The leadership style of the teacher affects the responsibility children take for their learning.

The *autocratic teacher* assumes all responsibility by defining all the classroom goals and rules and imposing them on the class. Autocratic leadership takes control and responsibility away from students and does not provide them with the skills to direct their own lives. A *laissez-faire teacher* takes little responsibility, allows almost complete freedom and establishes no clear goals. A laissez-faire approach does not provide for responsibility, cohesiveness, co-operative skills or academic achievement.

A *democratic teacher* in contrast, allows:

- Shared control and decision making with the class.
- Encouragement of group initiatives.
- Delegation of responsibility to the class.
- Working towards the establishment of mutual goals.
- Active participation in class activities.

Lewin's classic study (1948) illustrates some of the important differences between groups with different leadership styles. He found that the autocratic group functioned only when the leader was present. When the leader was absent the children quarrelled and were highly critical of each other. The laissez-faire group was chaotic. The democratic group, though, functioned well without the leader. The children were generally positive toward each other and behaved co-operatively. It is clear that without a democratic climate co-operative skills are unobtainable.

STRUCTURING SLOWLY FOR RESPONSIBILITY

By structuring the classroom carefully so that children slowly take on responsibility the teacher assumes the role of 'modern manager'. The modern manager does not coerce but rather explains his/her teaching role and responsibilities and within these parameters provides opportunities for children to make decisions. Responsibility is increased slowly so that children succeed at each step. By starting with a choice between two ideas and then adding more as they show they can handle it, the children assume responsibility for their own learning and develop appropriate classroom behaviour at their own pace.

RESPONSIBILITY FOR LEARNING

Children are interested and motivated learners when they are involved in decisions about what to learn and how to learn. They function best when goals are clearly articulated and attainable and the consequences or fall-back positions for not attaining the goals are decided jointly with the teacher. There are a range of different decisions children may make:

- setting goals for learning
- deciding on the means for achieving these goals
- deciding on the means for assessing achievements
- resetting goals after assessing achievements.

There are opportunities for children to make decisions about learning in small groups, as individuals and as a whole class. The process of group decision making requires negotiation and individuals may have to compromise. In order to reach group consensus children will need to put the skills for managing differences into practice.

RESPONSIBILITY FOR BEHAVIOUR

Traditionally teachers have taken responsibility for children's behaviour. Misbehaviour has been punished and worthy behaviour praised. Misbehaving children have usually been separated from the group. From the child's view, behaviour is generally directed by outside influences, such as teachers, parents and other children.

Approaches to discipline are clearly connected to teacher leadership style. These leadership styles also hold implications for the development of children's responsibility. The use of praise and punishment is linked to an autocratic style. However a more democratic leadership style encourages independence and demonstrates how behaviour is a choice.

This is an example of how it works.

Darren is in Year 3. He is very active and impulsive. When working or playing in groups he tries to take over. This often leads to arguments. Darren often ends up getting into trouble. Following one such incident Darren complained to the teacher.

Darren: 'It's not fair. I'm always getting in trouble.'
Mrs Fox: 'Why isn't it fair? Don't you deserve to get into trouble?'
Darren: 'Well, other people always make me angry.'
Mrs Fox: 'Other people make you angry? You don't have to behave angrily. You do have a choice about how you behave.'
Darren: 'What do you mean?'
Mrs Fox: 'Well, let's look at some other ways you could behave so you don't get into so much trouble.'

Darren agreed to this suggestion. The teacher and Darren worked out some alternative ways that Darren could react when he began to feel angry.

The following alternatives were suggested:

- count to ten
- explain how you are feeling

- look away at the sky or trees to make yourself relax
- ask the other person to stop
- move away
- ask yourself, 'Is it my turn or the other person's?'
- ask yourself, 'What is the person thinking?'

Over the next few days Darren showed that he could work in groups without getting angry. His teacher was quite surprised as she hadn't really believed that he could do it.

In the example Darren learnt to take responsibility for his own behaviour. The teacher provided him with alternatives and pointed out that the choice of behaviour was his own.

3

TEACHING

CO-OPERATIVE

SKILLS

Criticise the ideas and not the people.

Supporting children as they learn the co-operative skills, practise the skills and learn to give and receive feedback is a long-term commitment. For many classes a whole year could be spent on the simple skills of starting groups and learning how to work as a group. Other classes might move quickly onto quite complex problem solving as a group. The speed of progress usually depends on the amount of exposure children have had to co-operative skills and on their age and development. Some days children are more co-operative than others; sometimes after weeks of seeming to get nowhere the group begins to function beautifully. It takes all of one year to teach the skills well, and according to Johnson and Johnson (1986), sometimes up to two years before co-operative skills are second nature.

Just as we can demonstrate how to form letters, spell a word or punctuate a sentence, so too can co-operative skills be carefully taught. We often assume (mistakenly) that children know what's involved in co-operative activities when we suggest they 'Go into groups and construct a tower with blocks' or 'In a small group work out the best way to measure the playground.'

Observation of children often reveals one or two competent children doing the task while the others are 'hangers on', sometimes watching or otherwise engaged. The 'hangers on' would benefit from learning how to contribute to the group. The competent children, similarly, need to develop the social skills that enable them to include and involve others.

As we have mentioned in Chapter 2 the skills for working co-operatively in pairs or groups can be taught by making co-operative skills *explicit, practising* co-operative skills and giving *feedback*. These three components can occur daily. Some teachers set aside 15 minutes each day for demonstrating a particular skill and then have children practise it. Other teachers have become sold on the idea of co-operative learning and plan up to 75 per cent of the school day as pair or group activities where co-operative skills are taught, practised and monitored.

The following suggestions on how co-operative skills can be made explicit, practised and feedback given to a group are based on Johnson, Johnson and Holubec's important work (1986).

MAKING SKILLS EXPLICIT

Start by asking children what they do when they co-operate. List their ideas on a chart and add to it as more and more suggestions are forthcoming. To make these and other co-operative skills explicit, we can show examples of co-operative skills in action, use role play, read or tell stories from literature and build up T charts. These teaching strategies will now be discussed in more detail.

SHOWING EXAMPLES IN ACTION

Demonstrating co-operative skills in action in business, school committees and worldwide political negotiations can be arranged. The following suggestions illustrate the co-operative skills for starting groups, working as a group, problem solving and managing differences.

- Invite guest speakers who rely on co-operative skills do their jobs, e.g. the chairman of the school council, newspaper reporters, taxi drivers, supermarket workers etc.
- Use commercially produced playscripts or, better still, invent your own plays about family co-operation.
- Analyse charts or diagrams showing the links between co-operative group members.

The role of group recorder could be clarified first by discussing a picture of a citizens' action committee with a recorder or parliamentary reporter/court reporter in action. Then a list of duties the recorder performs could be brainstormed onto a chart for a future group recorder to follow. The complexity of each role and the co-operative skills to be practised depend on the age and experiences of the children.

ROLE PLAYING

Setting up role plays can occur quite spontaneously. For example, after children have been working as a group and have experienced difficulties co-operating the teacher can ask the group to try a particular activity

again. The others in the class can watch, sitting in a circle or fishbowl shape, and give feedback on the effectiveness of the co-operative skills. The group could then try it again, taking into account the suggestions from the class.

Most teachers find role play an excellent teaching technique, especially when they participate themselves. Take the starting group skill of taking turns, for example. The children in a Year 1 class were not sharing turns so the teacher sat on the floor with a group of two competent turn takers as they discussed what they did during the holidays. The teacher, with the two other children, practised taking turns in a goldfish bowl format with the role players in the centre and the rest of the class in a large semi-circle, watching. The rest of the class were riveted on the small group role play. They liked seeing the teacher as a group member and watching and working out how people make decisions about taking turns.

Writing the skill 'taking turns' on the blackboard cues the children in to the particular skill being practised. A list of behaviours the children observe can then be written up afterwards. We found that limiting the skills to one for each role play focuses the children's attention on that particular skill best of all.

DISCUSSING STORIES

Literary theorist Louise Rosenblatt (1978) and reading theorists such as Margaret Meek (1982) and Frank Smith (1978) agree that literature provides vicarious experiences for children and adults alike.

Although many books are based on the theme of individual wit and courage winning out over adversity, more and more books are now dealing with co-operation. Characters are helping each other to succeed in books such as *Space Demons* and *Skymaze* by Gillian Rubinstein, where children are reading that the group can achieve more than the individual.

In the picture book *Swimmy* by Leo Lionni a small fish joins with other small fish to make a huge fish shape to defeat a menacing shark. Careful questioning can help show children the ways the characters in these books co-operate, make decisions and solve conflict.

Appendix 3 (page 143) and Appendix 4 (page 145) have lists of co-operative books.

USING T CHARTS

T charts are a way of making co-operative behaviour explicit.

It is important to record what the behaviour looks like and sounds like as children who have not thought about what it means to take turns need strategies in the form of behaviour and words to ensure they get a turn. We have heard very shy children say, 'I watched your eyes carefully and asked if it was my turn but you did not give me a turn. It is my turn now!' Previously, this less assertive child would not have had the ideas and language to demand her right of a turn.

Taking turns	
Looks like	Sounds like
Nodding head	Have you finished?
Watching eyes	Is it my turn now?
Listening carefully	Can I say something now?

T charts can be displayed in the classroom to remind children what the co-operative behaviour looks like and sounds like.

PRACTISING CO-OPERATIVE SKILLS

There are continual opportunities for practising co-operative skills, but the best way to practise a new skill is to assign children a partner. In this way children can monitor their own use of co-operative skills without adding the complexity of big group numbers. Partner work can be practised each day in morning talks, maths or in any curriculum area where children are asked to share ideas.

Another useful and fun way to practise the skills is by playing co-operative games as 'warm-ups' to any lesson (see pages 113–24).

WORKING WITH A PARTNER

Once children have seen a role play, seen or heard about co-operation in action, or heard a story about taking turns and perhaps brainstormed a T chart, they can work in pairs to practise that co-operative skill.

Joan Dalton (1986) suggests that partner work can proceed in the following steps. The topic for partners to talk about could be 'What makes me scared.'

1. Children in pairs face each other.
2. Listener does not interrupt in any way.
3. Talker talks about 'What makes me scared.'
4. At a given signal the talker stops.
5. Listener reports main ideas from the talker to the class (only one or two listeners will have the time to report).
6. Children swap roles.

In this partner activity the forming group skills of one person speaking, using quiet voices, taking turns and looking at the speaker were practised and the group role of reporter was introduced.

The questioner

After lots of practice at taking turns, introduce the role of questioner. In pairs, the talker tells a story for example, 'The day the electricity stopped.' The listener/questioner works out two questions to ask the talker. The questions are to find out information the talker did not mention and can be who, what, when, why, where, or how questions. After two questions the roles can be swapped. (See Appendix 2, pages 125–42, for more partner ideas.)

GIVING FEEDBACK

'We don't have time to talk about how we work. Time is too short,' said Jane, exasperatedly.

Jane is a Year 6 teacher. She was feeling disgruntled because even though she structured her classroom program to include lots of co-operative activities the children still used put-downs and weren't helping each other in group activities. When she was asked what the children said about their use of put-downs and unco-operative behaviour she said they didn't have time to discuss it.

Setting time aside to provide feedback is one of the hardest things to remember to do but as Yager, Johnson and Johnson (1986) point out, feedback is as important as setting up the co-operative structures. They studied three groups of students: one co-operative group with time for feedback, one co-operative group with no feedback and a third group of students who all worked individually. The researchers monitored each group's productivity and found that the group that worked as individuals achieved least. The group that was encouraged to reflect on how the group worked and how it could be improved actually increased its productivity the longer it worked together. Up until three weeks after the unit of study, the group that provided itself with feedback was achieving more than the co-operative group that did not monitor and reflect on how it worked.

MAKING FEEDBACK CONSTRUCTIVE

Constructive feedback is important for several reasons. It provides information and the incentive to co-operate more effectively, be more efficient and remember to engage in co-operative skills.

An example worth analysing is that of a science unit in which children were inventing ways to keep a marble in motion for 8 seconds. An observer, Sally, was appointed to monitor how the group encouraged all members to contribute. The observer referred to the T chart on ways to encourage group members. A short observation chart with encouragement written on it was used to check off each time a group member encouraged someone.

At the conclusion of the activity Sally (8 years) said:

'Everyone in the group spoke. Sam asked people to share their ideas. I heard Tony praise Tod's idea to use cardboard. Everyone in the group gave an idea. Would you all give your opinion on how one other person encouraged someone and one idea about how we could improve?'

Sally had previously watched her teacher give feedback to a group and she knew to:

1. Focus on a person's behaviour and not his or her personality.
2. Describe what the person did, not what you think should have been done.
3. Avoid making judgements and using words like 'bad' or 'excellent.'
4. Be specific and concrete, not general and abstract.
5. Be brief and concise.
6. Give feedback immediately after the group activity.

The feedback Sally gave was constructive and non-threatening. She learnt this from her teacher who avoids negative feedback because it is so destructive when trying to build trust and cohesion in the classroom. This does not mean that classroom learning is always uncritical but rather that when feedback is given, it focuses on behaviour that has been observed. For example, Ms Sibenaler would say, 'People in the group encouraged each other five times,' rather than, 'Bill and Rebecca, you are always taking over and disrupting us.'

Negative feedback is to be avoided because:

1. Criticism carries more weight than does praise. One critical remark often outweighs dozens of positive comments.
2. People bring more to criticism than to praise because of their past history. Feelings from past criticism are tapped when criticism occurs in the present.
3. Trust is easy to destroy but hard to build. One sarcastic remark ridiculing children's behaviour can destroy trust built up over several weeks.
4. Weaknesses take more words to explain than do strengths. Describing what children do well is easier than looking for negatives.
5. Criticism confirms people's apprehension about being evaluated. Children will avoid being observed if they think it will result in negative criticism.

INTRODUCING FEEDBACK

Feedback works most effectively when the teacher plans ahead and selects what co-operative skills will be focused on. Starting out with the more simple co-operative skills like taking turns or encouraging seems to work best.

There are ten steps to keep in mind when beginning to give feedback (based on Johnson & Johnson 1988).

1. DECIDE ON THE SKILLS TO BE EMPHASISED

To begin a Year 3 class made a list of co-operative skills. The teacher then selected co-operative skills that she thought the children needed to practise. The ideas came from the co-operative skills for starting groups, working as a group, problem solving and managing differences.

She selected two skills to focus on for that week. The skills were incorporated into various curriculum areas such as maths where activity cards made the co-operative skill clearly explicit to the class, for example:

- Write down at least five ways to measure the oval.
- Each group member must contribute an idea.
- Group members *encourage* each other to give ideas.

Once the co-operative skill to be practised was decided the next step was to appoint an observer.

2. APPOINT AN OBSERVER

Teachers as first observer

The teacher is usually the first observer. She can model how an observer sits outside the group and does not contribute to the group discussion. (She is really 'invisible' and does not speak unless the group requests this.) Also the teacher can model how to give feedback that is constructive, specific and concrete.

Observers of pairs

An observer can be appointed to each pair or small group. It is more effective if children with well-developed co-operative skill are chosen first of all as they are usually clear about what to look for. Later observers who have fewer co-operative skills learn a lot from observing others practise the skills. For example, David interrupted when others were giving their ideas but once he had observed the group for taking turns he modified his behaviour and began waiting for his turn.

Roving observer

At times it is useful to have a roving observer looking at all the pairs or groups in action. The roving observer has an overview of how all groups are working and if this is the teacher she can intervene if necessary to ensure the groups are working co-operatively.

3. PREPARE OBSERVATION SHEETS

Using prepared observation sheets makes the role of observer quite formal but they are a must when beginning to teach observers what to look for. The use of observation forms makes all group members aware that they are being asked to contribute to the group work. Even very competent, co-operative groups may benefit from formal observation sheets if the group process becomes unsatisfactory and no one can pinpoint why. One school we know used observers in their staff meetings to make sure everyone was encouraged to participate.

The following page has examples of simple observation sheets:

Skill	Name	Name
One person speaks	Ted	Nonni

Gradually more skills can be introduced:

Skill	Name Sam	Name Jim	Name Soula
Taking turns Encourages ideas Gives idea			

or a simple tally of interactions can be recorded:

Encourages ☺	Questions ?

(See page 149 for a reproducible observation sheet.)

4. EXPLAIN THE FORMS

When introducing the observation sheet one teacher played the role of observer as two children shared their morning news. She had the observation form written on a large chart and the rest of the class watched as she recorded the number of times the pair encouraged each other. After this demonstration the children all formed pairs and an observer for each pair monitored the discussion using replicas of the form used by the teacher.

We have found that once children have used observation sheets once or twice little further explanation about them is necessary.

5. OBSERVING AND INTERVENING

The use of observation sheets helps make the observer more objective and produces evidence about what the group actually did. A careful observer will not confuse what the group did with interpretations and inferences, especially when observing friends. Observations should be descriptive not interpretive.

The following hints for using observation forms may be useful to tell children:

1. Mark the form each time you see someone use the particular skill being monitored.
2. Watch for non-verbal behaviours such as nods, eye contact, pointing and so on.
3. Don't worry if you can't record everything, just record as quickly as possible.
4. Make notes on the back of the sheet if what you want to record is not on the form.
5. Write down specific words or phrases to help you recall examples when you report your observations to the group.
6. Collect at least one positive action each member makes during the session.

Unstructured observations, where no forms are used, can also provide useful information to the group. Again specific behaviours and not interpretations can be jotted down so the group can receive specific feedback.

Intervention by the observer may be necessary if the group is not running smoothly. As a general rule though we find it best not to intervene unless things really get out of hand. Children also learn co-operative behaviour when they have to remedy poor group interactions by themselves. The idea of group responsibility for its efforts is endangered if the observer takes over.

6. ASSESS THE GROUP'S CO-OPERATION
Before the observer reports it is a good idea to have the group reflect on how they co-operated as individuals within the group. There are several ways of doing this:

- **Whip Technique**
  The teacher asks a specific question about how the group performed, for example, 'How did you encourage others?' or 'How were people's ideas built on?'. The group members then whip around the circle with 30 seconds to comment on a question. No other comments are allowed as the whip around must be quick.

- **Build-on whip**
  This is a quick whip around with each other member reporting on one behaviour that he or she performed that helped the group work effectively. Then the behaviour of the group member to the right (or left) is described. Again members have 30 seconds to report.

- **T chart report**
  Members refer to the T charts and comment on behaviours they used well from those listed on the T chart.

- **Questionnaire**
  Specially designed questionnaires can help group members focus on how well they worked on specific skills in the group, for example:

How did I work in the group?
Did I encourage another person?
Did I contribute ideas?
Did I help block a 'put-down'?
Did I criticise ideas and not people?
Did I help people stay on the task?

---

7. REPORTING TO THE GROUP
The way feedback is given is probably the most important factor in students' learning of co-operative skills. If feedback is positive it helps create energy to improve actions. Feedback allows children to fine-tune their

co-operative skills and corrects discrepancies between what they think they did and what was observed. It also helps clarify just what is involved in conducting a particular role or co-operative skill. For example, specific feedback on the skill of encouraging helps to clarify that behaviour:

'I heard people say encouraging things like...'

'I heard Tony ask Rob for his ideas.'

'I heard Sif encourage John by saying...'

When positive behaviour is recorded and given as feedback to the group the use of such behaviour is shown to be valued and encouraged. This works well if individuals each receive a positive comment:

'I saw Frank watch Susan's eyes as he waited for a turn.'

'I saw Domi keep his legs crossed and not touch anyone else.'

'I saw Sam look happy when Rob praised him.'

The observer, be it teacher or student, should take ownership for the feedback and make it personal by using 'I...' statements, such as 'I liked..'.

8. GROUP MEMBERS REFLECT

After hearing the observer's report group members need time to reflect on what can be improved. This can be done very quickly either by having each group member comment for 30 seconds or by giving the whole group a minute to reach consensus and decide on a group point of view.

9. COMPLIMENTING GROUP MEMBERS

There are lots of ways group members can compliment each other on their use of co-operative skills:

1. Focus on one member of the group. Each group member tells that person one thing they did that helped the group that day.

2. Distribute index cards with each group member's name written on the top. Group members write a positive comment about that person's effective use of co-operative skills. The cards are then given out so that every member will have positive feedback, in writing, from the group.

3. A list of beginning statements are given out and group members nominate another person to praise. The students then give these written statements to each other:

    'I appreciated it when you...'

    'I liked it when you...'

    'I enjoyed it when...'

    'You really helped us when...'

4. The list of beginning statements can be displayed in the classroom and group members give compliments orally.

Positive feedback is difficult for some children to accept. They find it hard at first to make eye contact while being complimented. Giving positive feedback can take time to develop and it takes time to learn to accept compliments without embarrassment.

10. SETTING GOALS

Setting goals to improve future co-operative work is the link between how students did today and how they will do tomorrow. The teacher may have general class goals for example:

'My class goal is to have quiet voices in group work.'

Individual class members can frame goals that fit in with the class goal but that are personal as well, for example:

'I will move to the group without talking.'

'I will only touch my own property.'

In this way both the teacher's class goals and the students' personal goals and desire for responsibility are fulfilled. Keep in mind that the goals that the students develop themselves provide much more incentive than teacher-imposed goals.

Other suggestions for setting goals include:

1. Students select and write down a goal to work towards in the next group session.
2. Each group or pair selects a group goal to work towards.

GROUP FEEDBACK	group A		
	yes	some times	no
Our group listened	*	(*)	*
We took turns	*	(*)	*
No put-downs	(*)	*	*
Encouraged everyone to speak	*	*	(*)

Our goal next time is to ....
.... Encourage everyone and
.... share
....

3. Contracts can be used, for example:

Name .... Date ....
Next time I will co-operate by ....
My goal is to practise .... by ....
My goal is to help the group by ....

4

FORMING GROUPS

*What makes us human is the way in which we
interact with other persons, and we learn how to
interact within the groups, in which we are
socialised and educated.*
— Johnson & Johnson

When we discuss initiating co-operative learning in groups with colleagues, the initial reaction is often something like, 'O.K. group work is fine. I always have people working in groups.' However there are important contrasts between co-operative learning and traditional grouping, which are outlined as follows:

1. Co-operative behaviour is encouraged by providing for positive interdependence. For example, asking children to form groups to discuss what they did on the weekend does not offer possibilities for positive interdependence, but asking one group member to report back with a summary of everyone's news means that all members have to cooperate. When all group members have to co-operate to perform the task they actively seek everyone's co-operation.

2. In addition to looking at content and the group product there is a focus on the group processes and the co-operative skills employed. Traditional grouping focuses mainly on content.

3. Co-operative skills are made explicit and practised. It is not just assumed that all children have the skills to work well together.

4. Children are provided with ways to observe and analyse their co-operative skills.

5. Children are provided with feedback about how well the group worked together. This feedback shows children that the quality of their interactions are valued. Children can be encouraged to set goals to continue to use these behaviours next time.

6. Equity issues are addressed in co-operative learning groups. Differences in gender, race, ethnicity and ability are combined in heterogeneous groups. Heterogeneous groupings provide greater opportunities for children to learn from others and promote cohesiveness in the classroom.

7. Co-operative learning may best suit the way girls learn, and boys benefit from learning co-operative skills.

8. Leadership roles are shared in co-operative groups. Children are often given specific roles which means less domination by a few in the group.

9. Co-operative groups de-emphasise the competition that can occur in traditional groupings.

HOW ONE TEACHER GOT STARTED

Ros had a ten-week employment contract teaching 5 and 6-year-old children at St Bernadette's School. She took up the contract in term four after working in country schools for several years.

On day one, Ros asked the children to go into groups. She found that some children co-operated well and others had a lot of difficulty. For example, Darren was working in a group of three and gazing into the air, banging his feet against a table when others spoke about what they would do for the forthcoming assembly. Ros spoke to him:

> Ros: 'Are you co-operating with your group?'
> Darren (looking puzzled): 'Yes.'
> Ros: 'What has the group decided to do for the assembly?'

Darren shrugged his shoulders and could not say. He continued bumping his feet against the table so that the other group members were distracted and kept on looking at him.

Darren did not see any need to co-operate. He did not have his goals for attention-seeking realised through co-operation and he did not have much idea about how to co-operate when or if he ever really needed to.

Although most of the children in the class could co-operate by talking and listening in their groups there were still many who had difficulty. Some didn't speak, some spoke all the time and one boy was so shy in class (not outside, by the way) that he did not make eye contact with the other children. This meant that he did not pick up on the clues from facial expressions that signalled his turn to speak. This very shy child was not from a background where direct eye contact is impolite. He had turned off.

Ros decided to demonstrate that all class members were valued, and to encourage their ideas. She began to teach co-operative skills in daily sessions. Ros asked the children to brainstorm what they do when they co-operate and made a list. Ros also added ideas. This list of co-operative skills became the basis for planning:

- making space for people
- making pairs or circles
- eye contact
- active listening
- staying with the group
- using quiet voices
- using people's names
- eliminating put-downs
- taking turns
- keeping hands and feet to yourself
- forming groups without bothering others

MAKING THE SKILLS EXPLICIT

Ros introduced the co-operative skill of taking turns by reading a picture book with a co-operative theme. She then discussed the particular skill and wrote 'taking turns' on a T chart.

Next Ros role played taking turns. She sat in the middle of a circle with Simon, a child chosen because of well-developed social skills. Ros and Simon talked about their weekend. After they had each had a turn they asked each other a question about something they wanted to know more about. The rest of the class sat in a fish bowl shape, observing.

The class then shared what it 'looks like' to take turns and what it 'sounds like' when people take turns. These ideas were recorded on the T chart.

Looks like	Sounds like
Eyes look at eyes. People wait until the talker has finished. Nodding head as you listen.	Have you finished? Do you want to say any more? That's interesting. That's great.

PRACTICE

Ros and the class then had a practice session. The children chose a partner and discussed their own news and asked questions of each other to ensure that positive interdependence was built in. This may sound very basic but for some children who say little and for those who say a lot it was not easy at all.

Ros walked around the room observing and as she did so she reminded the children that she was looking for taking turns. Some had already forgotten that this was the skill to be practised and had embarked on a long saga about their weekend, content to talk until all the time was up. At the end of this 5-minute session the children were asked to think about how they took turns and how their partners took turns. Each partner then told the other of one form of behaviour (from those listed on the T chart) that they did well. Ros then reported to everyone on what she saw working well.

MORE PRACTICE

Next day taking turns was discussed and children practised this skill but this time in teacher-assigned pairs. Watching the faces pulled when the children had to talk with someone of a different gender or someone who wasn't a close friend was very instructive. It is easy to take turns with friends but having to work or talk with others who are less familiar is hard for some children.

The tension created when gender, race and friendships were mixed presented a good opportunity to discuss the 'put-downs' that were heard such as 'Nerdface', 'You've got eyes like slits,' 'When I look at your face I think I'm going to be sick', 'I'm telling on you', 'You can't do tricks' and 'You're dumb.'

Ros made a list of 'Build-ups' and 'Put-downs'. Once these terms are brought out into the open they are easy to identify and build-ups are encouraged.

Build-ups and Put-downs

Ha ha you can't ride a bike.

You're a very nice person.

You can't say Christmas because you have gaps
in your teeth.

You're very good at riding a bike now.

I'm not your friend anymore.

You're lovable.

You're a stupid little boy.

You're pretty.

You're a strange person.

You're excellent.

I'm telling on you.

You do excellent work.

I hate you.

It's good you can tell the time now.

You're ugly.

You're my best friend.

You can't do tricks.

You are the best person I've met in years.

You eat grass.

You're good.

You eat snails.

You're generous.

You can't write.

GIVING FEEDBACK

Ros, like most of us, grew up in a competitive school system where the idea that one person will win and the rest will lose permeates all our thinking. It is easy to look for errors and to compare children. In the old competitive classroom one or two winners emerged and received most of the praise and constructive feedback.

In the co-operative classroom feedback on how the group worked co-operatively is important. Feedback is given on what a person did, on his or her behaviour, not statements about the individual's personality, for example:

'Jeremy encouraged others in his group.'

rather than

'Jeremy is such a nice, friendly person.'

Ros found that it is tempting to cut time set aside to give feedback from the program. But when time is allowed for feedback about how children have co-operated it demonstrates to the class that social skills and co-operation are valued. Feedback on the way people work is as important as the content being studied.

Ros worked on helping the children accept feedback. Sometimes talking about how Jeremy took turns or encouraged others sounded forced and false. When the teacher gave feedback it was easily accepted but when their peers complimented them the children often found it hard to take. Similarly, teachers find it hard to accept compliments from children and often squirm when a child says, 'I like your hair style', or 'You look good today.'

Perhaps we are not used to hearing positive feedback? Perhaps we are not used to describing social skills! Ros often had to say:

'It's good to hear how well we worked.'

'Look at the person when they are talking about how you worked.'

Ros encouraged the children not to be self-conscious but to think about their behaviour. As, Johnson, Johnson and Holubec (1988) remind us:

Whenever students feel awkward in engaging in the skill, when they feel phony, or when it feels mechanical, the immediate response by the teacher should be that more practice is needed... The goal for co-operative skill learning is to reach the stage where teachers can structure a lesson co-operatively and have students automatically and naturally engage in a high level of collaborative skills while achieving their learning goals. (p.5:19).

USING OBSERVERS

Ros found that selecting children to act as observers was the best way to get feedback on the use of co-operative skills. She asked observers to look out for specific behaviour and this immediately alerted not only the observer but also the whole group to the kind of behaviour that was to be observed. Group co-operation suddenly improved dramatically. The skills being looked for included encouraging, taking turns and using quiet voices. One skill was given in the first session then more skills were added gradually.

Ros used cards, labelled with the word 'observer', on string to slip over a child's head. This made it clear who was playing the role of observer and group member. She also duplicated observation sheets so that the skill could be added quickly and the observer could get to work. (See photocopiable sheets on pages 149–52.)

SAMPLE LESSON
INTRODUCING THE ROLE OF OBSERVER

1. **Curriculum area:** All

   Lesson Objectives: To introduce the role of observer and practise listening and speaking.
   Materials: Butcher's paper for a T chart, marker pens, observation sheet.

2. **What kind of group?**: Work in pairs, teacher selected, with an observer
   Roles: Appoint an observer.

3. **The lesson**: 'I read the book *I Do Not Like It When My Friend Comes to Visit*, by Ivan Sherman. We then talked about friendship and sharing things. Next we discussed ways we could encourage each other to share ideas, to help with the group work and to feel good about ourselves. Then we made a T chart and the children described what encouragement can look like and sound like.'

Encouragement Sounds like	Looks like
Good idea	Nods head
Great	Uses hands to encourage
I like that idea	Smiles
O.K.	Raises eyebrows
Good	Opens eyes wide
Yes, anything else?	Shows interest

Next, a role play between two children was used to demonstrate how the observer's role worked. Ros was the observer and used a blown-up version of the observation sheet. While the two children talked about what favourite TV programs they had in common, the teacher checked off when encouragement was used.

At the conclusion of the role play the kinds of encouragement the children used were described. Children commented on what they saw and what they heard as encouragement.

Next, student observers were selected and given an observation sheet. Children talked in pairs on the same topic. An observer watched, then reported to the pair on how they encouraged each other.

Positive interdependence: Pairs have to come up with ideas that both share.

Feedback and reflection: The observers all report back to the pair. The teacher also shares what she has observed. (Make sure the report back doesn't become a competition.)

Comment: If the observers are told they are invisible this stops them from interrupting the discussion. Also, even though the observers report to their group, it is a good idea to come back as a class and have one or two observers describe what their group did. In this way the role of the observer is further clarified.

Co-operation takes time and practice. Ros says there are lots of questions to keep in mind when planning for co-operation:

- Is there a shared group goal?
- Do all group members have to co-operate to reach the goal?
- Will all group members see their role in the group as important?
- How will the feedback the teacher gives ensure that positive interdependence and not individual competition is stressed and valued?
- Will the teacher give some form of group assessment this time?
- Will the groups assess how they worked together?

Ros concludes:

'Most of us have avoided comparing children on the basis of academic ability for years. We don't say, "Jimmy knows more about maths than you, Sam." Yet we still compare children's social skills and set up competitive situations. Our language in the classroom often includes comments like, "Paul's group was first", "Sally tries harder than you". Competition and comparing children for social skills still occurs. There is lots of work to be done.'

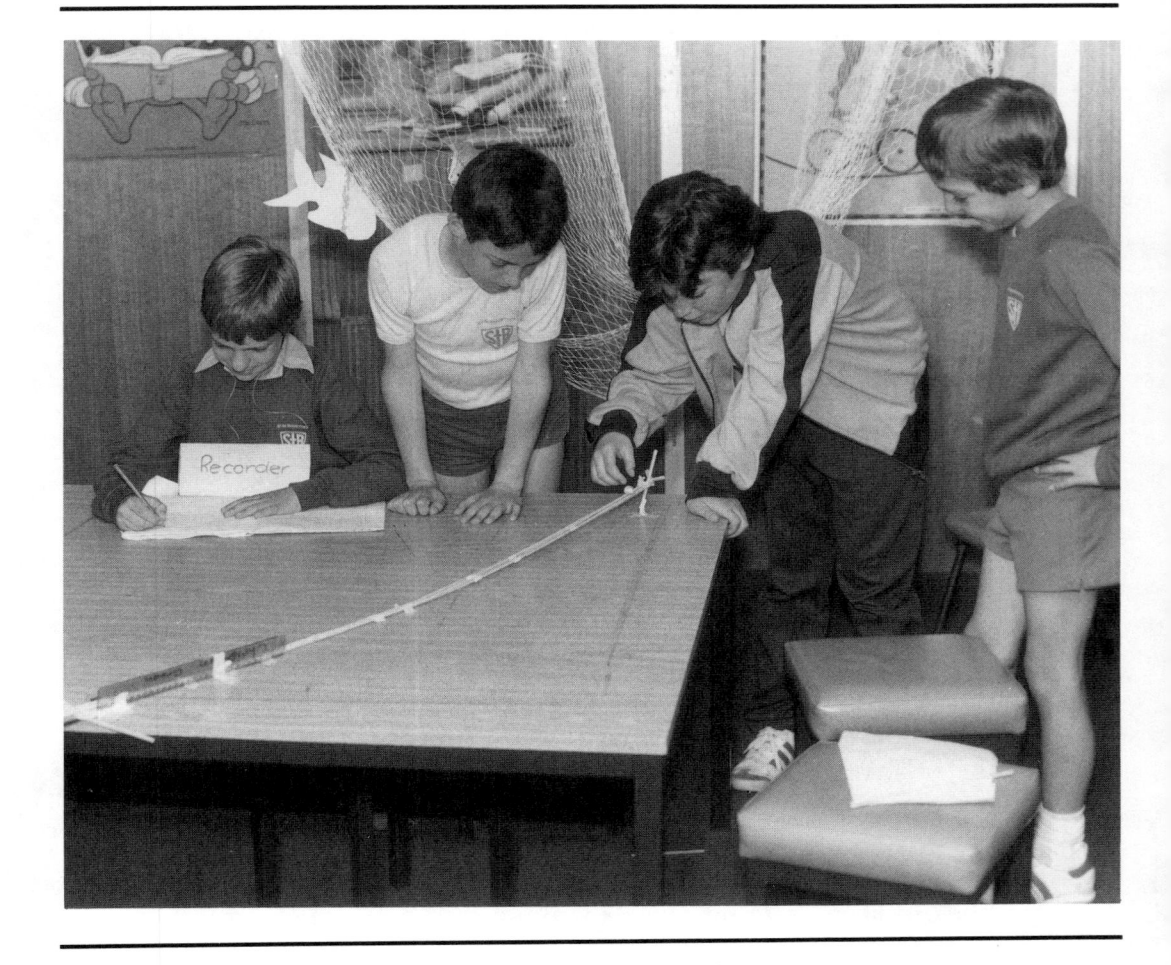

5

WORKING

AS A GROUP

Leadership roles are easily taught. When beginning group work the role of observer is the first one to learn; the observer can be introduced as soon as children are comfortable with partner work.

The same procedure for making explicit the co-operative skills for starting groups is again used for teaching group roles. First show the roles in operation, for example, in role plays. Then build up T charts about what each leadership role 'sounds like' and 'looks like'. Practice and feedback on the effectiveness of the roles then continue.

Leadership roles can include:

Observer: Watches the group and gives feedback on co-operative skills. The observer is 'invisible' to the group and rarely intervenes in the group discussion. Examples of observer comments include:

'Linda asked for other people's ideas.'

'I counted six blocks to put-downs.'

'Everyone made space for the group.'

Summariser: Retells main ideas, e.g.:

'The group said that we should...'

'Two people thought that...and one did not.'

'Most people took holidays at...and did these things...'

'We can't decide until we have heard what everyone thinks.'

Recorder: Writes down the group ideas, e.g.:

'Is this what you said?'

'How shall I write that...?'

Encourager: Encourages, seeks others' ideas, builds others' self-esteem, e.g.:

'That's a good point.'

'You really helped me a lot by explaining that.'

'Has everyone had a turn?'

Clarifier: Asks if the group understands, explains ideas, links ideas, asks for evidence/explanation, paraphrases, e.g.:

'Did anyone have a problem with those words?'

'That idea is like Simon's first suggestion.'

'Another way to say that is...'

'Can you say it another way?'

'How do you know that is true?'

Organiser: Keeps people on the task, repeats the problem to be solved, reminds people of their roles, shows people where they agree, mediates, e.g.:

'The problem is...that idea is off the track.'

'We have to come up with a response to tell the others.'

'You both agree on this point.'

'Can the recorder take down that idea?'

Challenger: Stirs up thinking, takes a different point of view, e.g.:

'Is there another way to look at this?'

'Isn't that just taking the easy way out?'

'Will that suggestion really help?'

Time-keeper: Watches time, tells when time is nearly up.

'I will let you know when time is nearly up.'

'We have five minutes.'

These were some beginning roles. Other roles were added later, such as:

Questioner: Forms open-ended questions for the group:

'If you were in that position what would you do?'

'Could this story be true? How would you know if it was or wasn't?'

Predictor: Asks the group to predict all the possible outcomes, especially in reading and project work:

'Look at the cover of the book. What do you think it will be about?'

'Who will the characters be?'

'What will happen to them?'

ACTIVITIES FOR PRACTISING GROUP ROLES

ROLE PLAY GAME*

One way to help children see the importance of co-operative group roles is to have them view unhelpful roles in practice. Make four cards with the following role descriptions written on the front.

BOSS

Always tries to take over and has to be in charge.

Puts down other people's ideas and doesn't listen.

Says • Listen to me. I know.
  • My way is best.
  • I don't think that idea is as good as mine.
  • Do it my way or else.

DESTROYER

Sets out to wreck the co-operative spirit in the group.

Makes fun and demeans the task. Looks bored.

Says • This is stupid, it's just a waste of time.
  • I don't want to do this.
  • None of our ideas will ever work.
  • You are all so boring.

---

*Adapted from Pike and Selby (1988)

SHOW-OFF

Tries to get attention in any way at all. Jumps from topic to topic to keep the attention. Fiddles, tells jokes and tries to catch other people's eyes at all times.

Says • Look what I just did.
  • Why are you being so serious?
  • Have you heard this one?
  • Can you do this with your eyes?

CRAWLER

Always praising but for no apparent reason.

Says • Oh, Jane always has the good ideas.
  • I wish I was clever like you.
  • You just say it so well.
  • I was just going to say that. We always agree.

Put the cards into a hat. Ask four volunteers to pick a card (but not show anyone their card), read their role silently and play that role in a group discussion. The rest of the class watches, sitting in a fishbowl shape, and tries to identify the various roles.

Some topics for the group to discuss could be:

• The three most popular foods liked by all in the group.
• Rank the three best rock 'n' roll groups.
• What two TV stars would you like to invite to the school?

Set a time limit of 5 minutes for discussion.

Ask children if they recognise any similarities between the roles the group is playing and behaviour they have seen. Ask them if they recognise any behaviour that is similar to their own. Ask if there is some part of their own group behaviour that could be improved. Ask if they can name the unhelpful roles they just witnessed.

Now make another four cards with helpful roles on them:

ENCOURAGER

Encourages and builds self-esteem of others when deserved. Asks others for their ideas.

Says • That's a good point.
  • Has everyone had a turn?
  • You really helped me by saying that.

ORGANISER

Keeps people on task, repeats the problem to be solved, shows people where they agree, mediates.

Says • The problem is...That is not related to the issue.
  • We have to come up with a response.
  • You seem to agree (here) and (here).

SUMMARISER

Retells all the main ideas from the group.

Says • The group said...
  • We can't make a decision until everyone has contributed and all the ideas have been heard.
  • Two people thought...and one did not.

CLARIFIER

Asks if the group understands. Explains ideas, links ideas, asks for evidence/explanation, paraphrases.

Says • Did everyone understand that?
  • That idea is like Simon's idea.
  • Can you say that another way?
  • How do you know that is true?

Put the helpful and unhelpful cards in two 'hats'. In groups of four, two people pull out helpful roles and two pull out unhelpful roles, but they don't show anyone else the role card.

They then discuss one of the topics given above or any topic calling for agreement or ranking of items. The children discuss the group roles and have to try to identify who was who.

This game can be played whenever groups need to be reminded about helpful roles. Teacher follow-up is essential so that clarification of what the roles entail is absolutely clear. The cards describing the roles can be displayed in the classroom for the children to refer to when practising group roles at other times.

SAMPLE LESSONS
GROUP TALKS
1. Curriculum area: All

2. Kind of group: Four children in a group, teacher-assigned groups with mixed gender, race and ability.

Roles: Summariser retells the main ideas and reports back to the whole group.

Materials: Teacher-made cards with open-ended questions relating to human rights.

```
        How would I put the world right?
```

```
            What is prejudice?
            How does it occur?
            What can we do about it?
```

```
        What are the needs and rights of children?
```

3. The lesson: 'Today we are continuing to think about the basic human rights that everyone deserves. In groups of four talk about one of these topics (number off the twenty-four children). I will read out each topic.' (There are several copies of each card so that each group has a card.) 'One person will summarise the main ideas from each group and report back.' (Nominate summariser).

Positive interdependence: All the main ideas from each group member are used in the summary.

4. Feedback and reflection: The teacher monitors the children's ability to summarise ideas and not just repeat all the details.

Comment: A card with the word summariser was worn around the summariser's neck. This helped to clarify the specific summariser role for other group members.

ROLE READING

1. Curriculum area: Language/reading

2. Kind of group: Groups of four. In the group the teacher plays various roles to demonstrate procedures while the class watches. Once the group is familiar with the procedures the teacher leaves the group.

This could take between two to six sessions and the teacher could play several different roles to make sure the children understand. The more familiar the children are with taking roles the quicker they will move into this activity. It then works very, very well. (Cathy's class picked it up in two sessions.)

Roles:

Predictor/
Recorder: Asks the group to predict, in turn, what they think the story will be about. These predictions can be recorded on paper.

Summariser: Retells main ideas about what has been read.

Questioner: Generates a question(s) for the group to answer.

Clarifier: Asks the group if they understand the ideas in the reading. This is only done if there is the possibility of confusion. It should not be routine.

Roles are changed after each session to share the leadership roles. **Materials:** There should be copies of a text for all to read silently. Big books can be used but small books, one between two, work well. Fiction or non-fiction works equally well as a text and it really depends on what the group is interested in reading at the time.
The lesson: 'Today we are going to continue to find out about human rights. We will be reading about human rights in South Africa. We will all have a role to play. Today I will be the predictor.

Jim, will you be the summariser and retell the main ideas from the reading?

Rebecca, will you read the passage and work out a question for the group to answer? You will be the questioner and the question should not just have a yes/no answer but encourage the group to have differing opinions.

Sally, will you be the clarifier and check that everyone understands what we are reading?' (More information is given so that children are clear about their roles. The teacher coaches children in their roles for as long as necessary.)

Step 1: Prediction

'First let's think about what human rights means. We'll write this down in a brainstormed list. Now let's predict what the passage we are going to read will be about. The title is Human Rights in South Africa.' All the group members are invited to predict what they will read. At times the predictor could write this down so the group can check their predictions.

Step 2: Read

'Now let's all read silently and see if our predictions are correct.' A short article is best to begin with. In getting the groups started a paragraph at a time works best. Reading a paragraph at a time also works well if the material is dense with complex ideas.

Step 3: Summarise

The summariser now retells the main ideas read.

Step 4: Question

The questioner asks the group an open-ended question. Interpretive, critical or creative questions are asked.

Step 5: Clarify

The clarifier asks if anyone had any problems understanding the text, the vocabulary or the questions.

Step 1: Prediction (repeat Step 1)

The predictor asks the group to predict what the next section will be about. The process is continued until the whole text has been read.

Positive interdependence: The designated roles create positive inter-pendence as all group members have an interdependent role to play.

Feedback and reflection: For feedback use examples of how students used roles to help the group work co-operatively, for example:

> 'Jim made sure that everyone who had a prediction had a chance to tell us.'

or

> 'Sam asked open-ended questions that made us think about why the author wrote about human rights.'

Comments: The teacher role plays or models how to engage in the roles of summariser, predictor, clarifier and questioner. When starting it is best to work with one group of fluent readers. These readers can then go into other groups and teach other children what to do. Mixed ability groups seem to work well. The most demanding roles are summariser and questioner, so assign the most proficient readers to these roles.

It helps the children remember the role they are playing if cards or buttons are made with the various roles named clearly on the front. **Note: Big books work very effectively for role reading.**

MATHEMATICS

1. Curriculum area: Maths.

2. Kind of group: Four children in a group, teacher assigned with mixed abilities.

Roles: Assign roles of:

- recorder
- observer (observation sheet prepared)
- questioner
- organiser

Materials: Mathematics cards are written for each group. These cards can be used in two different ways.

1. The whole class completes the cards, one at a time, in groups. The findings of the different groups are shared by all in the class.

2. Groups of four rotate through the cards, engaging in one activity for several sessions or over the entire week.
   These are three examples of cards you could work with.

Party plan

You are organising a party to celebrate the end of term. How are you going to do this? In your group consider:

- the cost
- when to hold it
- whom to invite
- where to hold the party
- how it will be organised
- what will happen at the party

Organiser .... Recorder ....

Observer .... Questioner ....

Board game

A major game publisher invites you to design and submit a board game in which the mathematical concepts **+**, **−**, **×** and **÷** are used somewhere in the game. Make a model of the game and write instructions under these headings:

Aim of the game   *Materials needed*

Players

Observer ....

Take a holiday

Organise a holiday for your group. You could go overseas or stay locally. You have $15,000 to spend, donated by an old scholar of the school. Consider:

- Where to go?
- How to get there?
- What will different parts of the journey cost?
- Where will you begin or end?
- What will your itinerary be?
- How will you travel?
- How much will you spend?
- Will you need insurance?

Observer .... Questioner ....

Organiser .... Recorder ....

Use pamphlets from the Tourist Bureau to help you complete the assignment.

Feedback and reflection: As well as sharing the findings from each group on the ways they solved the mathematical problems the observer can report back on how the group co-operated. Individuals can also reflect on their own co-operative skills.

SOCIAL STUDIES

In investigating the question, 'Where did we come from?' children can work in co-operative groups.

Kind of group: Groups of four with names selected randomly. It is important that children do not just go with their friends but work with other people in the class.

Roles:

Summariser: Puts all the ideas together. Retells the main ideas to the group and the whole class.

Recorder: Writes down all the main ideas the group thinks are important to record.

Encourager: Supports others by encouraging their contributions when the contributions add to the discussion. Can encourage everyone to contribute ideas.

Organiser: Watches the time and reminds people to stick to the task.

Materials: A list of different ethnic groups. Reference books, atlas, maps, tourist brochures and a list of people living in the area or attached to the school who have recently migrated to Australia. Paper, pens, tape recorder. Cards with tasks clearly outlined:

Find out where the people who migrated to Australia came from. Plan a trip to each of the countries you found. How would you get to that country?

Find out why people came to Australia. Prepare an interview form and interview a person who recently arrived here.

What differences exist between an Australian celebration and a celebration in another country? What is the same about some celebrations?

Plan a menu for a party for the class where the food comes from at least five or more different countries. Make sure the recipes are easy to make.

How do people live in different countries? Prepare an interview form and interview two people who were born in countries outside Australia.

READERS THEATRE

Subject: Drama

Objectives: Take a well-known chant or rhyme and read it aloud in a group. Use variety in pitch, volume and expression.

Materials: Copies of poems/rhymes, for the group to make a selection of one to practise for performance.

Group decision: Divide the class into groups of six to eight of mixed gender and reading ability.

Roles:

Director: Develops reading expression, pace of reading, helps polish reading for performance.

Producer: Selects readers, organises rehearsals.

Checker: Checks that people come in on time, records notes on paper to help performance if necessary.

Special effects: Decides on music or other accompaniment.

The lesson: 'Take a poem from those provided. Select one that your group could practise and polish for a classroom performance. Add claps, clicks, sound effects if necessary. Those people who do not have the roles of director, producer, checker or special effects are to observe how the group encourages all to participate. You have 30 minutes to practise your piece.'

Positive interdependence: All the children must co-operate to make the show a success.

Feedback and reflection: Talk about roles played co-operatively.

End of session: Have everyone view the readers theatre performances. Discuss the co-operative skills that people used.

LANGUAGE

Order in the court

Objectives: The children form arguments to support a position.

Materials: Role cards are needed and these are put around the players' necks.

Kind of group: Divide the class into heterogeneous groups of five.

Roles: Assign roles

Juror:	Listens to the cases for and against. Votes guilty or not guilty.
Judge:	Keeps order, asks for clarification, decides with the jury's help who is guilty and who is not.
Defendant:	Makes a clever argument to defend the accused.

Prosecutor:	Makes a case against the accused.
Accused:	Accused of the crime. May be guilty, may be not guilty. Cannot speak unless called to speak by the defendant or prosecutor.

The lesson: 'Today we are going to learn how a court works. I'll be the defendant who defends the accused by making up a believable case to show why she/he is not guilty.' (The teacher then assigns students to the various roles. The court procedure is practised in a goldfish bowl style with the rest of the class watching. If the roles and their explanation are written on the blackboard the children can refer to what they can do.) 'The activity will last for 15 minutes. The judge will be the time-keeper. The accused is alleged to have stolen from...'

Positive interdependence: Once the children are assigned roles the group process is positively interdependent. All are dependent on each other. Feedback monitor for taking turns and timing so all have a turn to speak.

6

PROBLEM SOLVING

*Not everything that is faced can be changed but
nothing can be changed until it is faced.*
— James Baldwin

There are many co-operative skills that children can learn in order to work effectively in groups to solve problems. The skills for problem solving include and build upon the skills for working as a group. For example, Tony and Neil had decided to write a funny story together, on a topic of their own choice. After questions — 'What will we write about?', 'How will we start?' — they decided to brainstorm a list of topics then agree on one topic that they both liked. They picked a topic that was to be a send-up of funny characters in a TV show. Then they said, 'If we take the idea of the "Alf" how can we make it sound a bit different from the TV show?'

A list of ideas was brainstormed and alternative solutions to problems were given. The discussion proceeded in this manner. As the boys continued writing, the process of identifying problems, brainstorming alternative solutions and selecting an agreeable solution was repeated continually until the piece was finished.

The skills of arguing constructively about problems, finding alternative solutions, and then agreeing on one solution are an important part of group problem solving. When engaged in problem solving children have to explain their ideas or their position. This discussion stimulates thinking and promotes learning.

There are several steps that can be used in problem solving:

1. **Defining the problem**
   What is the problem? Sometimes the central issues are clear. However, at other times it is difficult to delineate what the problem really is. Sometimes personal values and attitudes affect the way in which a

problem is interpreted. Thus it may be necessary for the group to ensure that all members understand the problem in the same way. Often it becomes clear that there are different conceptions of the problem only after the group has been working on it for some time.

2. **Collecting information**

Relevant facts, opinions and values will need to be collected.

3. **Analysing data**

This involves the group in trying out ideas, eliminating the irrelevant content, experimenting, choosing, drawing maps or graphic outlines of how ideas fit together.

4. **Selecting a solution**

Some problems have only a single solution, i.e. they are either right or wrong. Where the problem is open-ended the group needs to establish criteria for selecting the best alternative. It may be appropriate for the group to select a number of alternative solutions.

5. **Testing a solution**

The group may have an opportunity to test out its solution.

6. **Evaluating the solution**

The solution can be evaluated by the group. If the solution doesn't work then the process of problem solving starts again.

A number of important co-operative skills are used by groups when solving problems. Problem solving is not a lock-step process where each skill is used in order. At all stages of problem solving the group may need to modify its decisions and circle back to earlier steps of the problem-solving process.

DEFINING THE PROBLEM

The problem could be set by the teacher: 'Your group could make a play about the book' or 'Find ways to measure...'. Alternatively the group could come up with a problem to solve, for example, 'Let's make a vegetable garden', 'Let's have a class party'. Spending time to define the problem carefully saves wasted time later.

The group can consider whether a question or problem is one it really wants to pursue. Once the decision has been made to proceed, it is helpful to lay out all the known facts about the problem or question. A list of what you know and what you need to know is helpful.

What we know	What we need to know

Checklists like who, what, where, when, why and how help clarify the problem. After time spent defining the problem carefully the group can move to brainstorming solutions.

BRAINSTORMING

Brainstorming is a very useful way of getting a large number of ideas from a group of people in a short amount of time. Brainstorming is particularly useful after a problem has been defined, but it can be employed at any stage of the problem-solving process.

Brainstorming involves listing ideas without making any evaluative judgements. Wild and silly ideas are encouraged. Only after a list of ideas has been brainstormed and recorded should the group begin to make judgements about ideas suggested.

When brainstorming, all those in the group are asked to make immediate responses to ways to solve the problem, topic or issue. All responses are listed on the board or a chart.

The guidelines for brainstorming can be displayed in the classroom.

Brainstorming Guidelines
1. All ideas are accepted and written down.
2. There should be no evaluative comments (positive or negative).
3. Offer ideas even if you are unsure about them.
4. Build on other people's ideas.

HOW LONG?

The group may set a specific time aside for brainstorming or agree to stop only when the flow of ideas begins to slow down. Brainstorming can last from 5 minutes to 30 minutes.

GROUP SIZE

If the group is bigger than twenty it will be hard for everyone to have a say. Split large groups into two or three smaller groups, each with a recorder. Groups of four may be quiet and not as forthcoming as groups of six to eight members. At other times groups of two or three can work very effectively brainstorming ideas to research or write about. Mix up the group membership so that girls, boys, and children of differing abilities and interests are used to enrich and stimulate ideas.

RECORDING IDEAS

The recorder should not 'put down' or leave out any ideas. If the recorder is the teacher it is important to leave evaluation of ideas to a later stage. If ideas are recorded on newsprint charts they can be stored and used later. To help discussion of the ideas the recorder should number each point.

WHAT TO DO WHEN IDEAS DRY UP

As a brainstorming session continues the flow of ideas will fluctuate. After an initial fast flow the rate will slow down. To generate new ideas try these:
- One minute of silent thinking.
- Reread the list of ideas.
- Try a subtopic. If children are brainstorming ideas about sea life try extending ideas on the subtopic of dolphins. Or when brainstorming words to use in a poem, smaller groups can be formed to brainstorm subtopics such as political words, emotional words and rhyming words.
- Use a brainstorming warm-up to get ideas flowing: 'How many ways can you use a rubber boot?' or 'Suppose you woke up and you were 2 metres tall, what would you do?' Don't record these ideas. They are just used to free up ideas.
- Don't use an observer as this dries up a brainstorm.

FINISHING UP

Finish by asking the group for some really wild ideas. Sometimes it is these ideas that end up being the best for solving a problem.

Brainstorming has many advantages as it:
- minimises conflict within a group. As everyone offers ideas the suggestions become the property of the group as a whole and not of individual group members.
- encourages everybody to take part and helps develop cohesiveness in the group.
- encourages creative thinking.

Almost any open-ended question provides a good topic for brainstorming, for example:
- How can we reduce the road toll?
- Who would you like to visit and talk to the class?
- What forms of communication will be available in fifty years' time?
- What are some things that we could do to raise money for books?

VARIATIONS

CUBING

Students look at a problem from six different sides. If the topic is 'junk food in the tuckshop' the group can discuss the issue using six sides or viewpoints. The technique of cubing can also be used in brainstorming writing once a topic has been selected:
- Describe it (Describe its colour, shape, size.)
- Compare it (What is it similar to or different from?)
- Associate it (What does it make you think of?)
- Analyse it (What is it made up of?)
- Apply it (What can you do with it? How can it be used?)
- Argue for or against it (Take a stand and list reasons supporting it.)

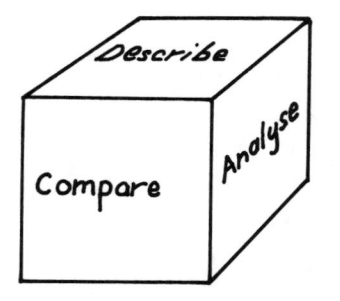

ATTRIBUTE LISTING

Take a topic and list all of its attributes. Take the topic group ball games, for example. Now list all the attributes including size, shape, colour, weight, function and so on for ball games. Then concentrate on one attribute that might be changed or improved.

If problems occur in the playground at recess all the attributes of recess can be listed (time, place, games, purpose, people) and the group can brainstorm improvements to each of these attributes.

FORCED RELATIONSHIPS

This idea is best explained by using a grid. Across the top list a series of ideas and down the side other ideas are listed. Say you want to write a story — you could list characters down the side; across the top list goals, obstacles and results. This provides a whole range of ideas for narrative writing, for example:

	Events	Goals	Obstacles	Events	Resolution	Theme
Characters						
robber						
wife						
frog						
giraffe						
king						

	limp	lumpy	loose	luscious	little	
lemons						
lavender						
lentils						
loaf						
leaf						

CHECKLISTS

Take a problem such as getting more playground equipment. Using this checklist the problem can be explored further.

```
Adapt?
Modify?
Put things to other uses?
Magnify?
Minify?
Substitute?
Rearrange?
Reverse?
Combine?
```

Students can create other checklists to jog their thinking. A checklist to use for brainstorming ideas or coming up with answers to problems is 'who, what, when, why, where and how?'.

CLARIFYING IDEAS

Clarifying is necessary when the problem is not understood or there is uncertainty about what has been said or simply more information is needed. When working as a group the role of clarifier is to check whether other group members understand or need more information. However when groups are engaged in creative problem solving then all members should be skilled at asking appropriate questions to clarify what has been said.

Questions for clarification might be:

'I'm unclear about that. Tell me what you mean?'

'Could you tell me more about that?'

'Why did you say that?'

'How do you know that is true?'

'In how many situations could that be used?'

CONFIRMING IDEAS

Group members use this skill to make sure they understand what is being said. Confirming is a way of checking that you have the same idea as the speaker. It also shows the speaker that you understand what has been said. Confirming is an important skill that reflects active listening. (See Appendix 2, pages 129–31 for activities for attentive listening.) There is a natural tendency for all of us to evaluate a person's idea immediately

or to make an assumption about what is being said without actively listening and checking back to confirm ideas.

The skill of confirming ideas requires the listener to stop and assume that there is something of value in what is being said without immediately trying to judge the idea. In order to confirm or make sure you understand what the speaker has said you might:

Paraphrase the idea:

'In other words you're saying...'

Repeat the statement word for word:

'Your idea is that...'

Say that you understand exactly what has been said:

'I understand that you believe that...'

ELABORATING

A further important skill when discussing problems is the ability to build on or elaborate the ideas offered by others. Elaborating enables a group to develop better and more creative ideas or solutions to problems. When people see how an idea can be applied to a different situation or how an idea can be refined or improved they use the skill of elaborating.

When building on another's ideas children can point out the connection between the original idea and their own idea. The next step is to check back with the person to make sure the ideas are consistent with the original point. In this way the originator of the idea is clearly acknowledged and confirmation is also sought.

```
                    Acknowledge first idea
                              |
                         Elaborate
                              |
                       Confirm ideas
```

For example the group may be discussing where to go for a school camp. One suggestion is:

'Let's go to the mountains because there are places to do bushwalking.'
To elaborate on this someone could say:
'Yes, we could go to the mountains like...[name] said' (*acknowledge ideas*)
'and we could stay at the hostel at the base of the mountains.' (*elaborate*)
'do you agree[name]?' (*confirm*)

SEEING CONSEQUENCES

After the group has brainstormed, clarified, confirmed and elaborated on ideas and solutions to problems, it is useful to predict consequences that might result from each solution.

This is how one group proceeded:

Problem

You are backpacking and can carry one type of food. Your friend is a vegetarian. You love barbecues.

Solutions	Consequences
1. You could do without meat for one day.	Not fair because meat gives you the energy you need.
2. You both could eat what you want.	Both would be happy but there would be extra weight to carry.
3. Get a new friend.	No, you have been friends for years.

4. Cancel the trip.   Not worth cancelling it.
5. Go on a different trip to your friend.   Then both could eat what they like.

Choose a solution. Both 2 and 5 seem reasonable but the second solution would suit both even though there would be more to carry.

CRITICISING IDEAS

When problem solving as a group the use of constructive criticism is very important. Group members have to learn not to be defensive or to take criticism personally. For criticism to be constructive it must be specific. In other words 'I don't like that' or 'That's no good' does not provide any useful information. If statements such as these are made they can be ignored unless the person can be more specific and describe what he or she doesn't like.

When making criticism in a constructive way students can be encouraged to first suggest points with which they agree and then be specific about those points of which they are critical.

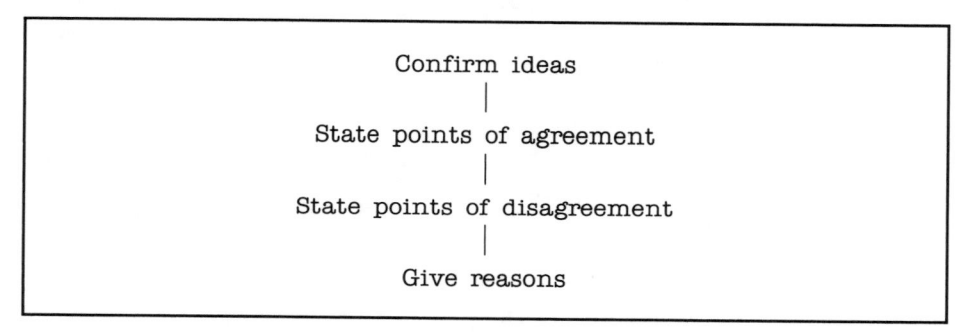

Confirm ideas
|
State points of agreement
|
State points of disagreement
|
Give reasons

A group may have been set a task of deciding what cooking equipment to take on a camp. One group member says:
'We should only take basic cooking equipment, like a billy and a pan to use over a fire. Too much gear will be too heavy to carry.'
Another member of the group criticises constructively by saying:
'I agree that too much equipment could be heavy but if we took a gas fire we could cook if it rains.'
Constructive criticism includes confirmation points of agreement and points of disagreement and provides a reason for the disagreement.

ORGANISING INFORMATION

When a group has collected a variety of loosely connected ideas some time needs to be spent organising them. The central notion when organising information is finding common elements that exist in different suggestions or ideas. For example, the group might display all the brain-stormed ideas for equipment to take on a camp. Then, by looking for common elements like cooking gear or sleeping gear, they find all ideas can be organised into four different categories.

Organising information represents an important problem-solving skill in itself and there is no one correct way to do it. It allows children to structure, interpret and represent information without a structure imposed upon them.

One useful way to proceed is to put ideas or concepts into a diagram. Boxes or circles can be used. Lines can be drawn to show relationships.

GRAPHIC OUTLINES

Graphic outlines show the relationships between ideas in diagrammatic form:

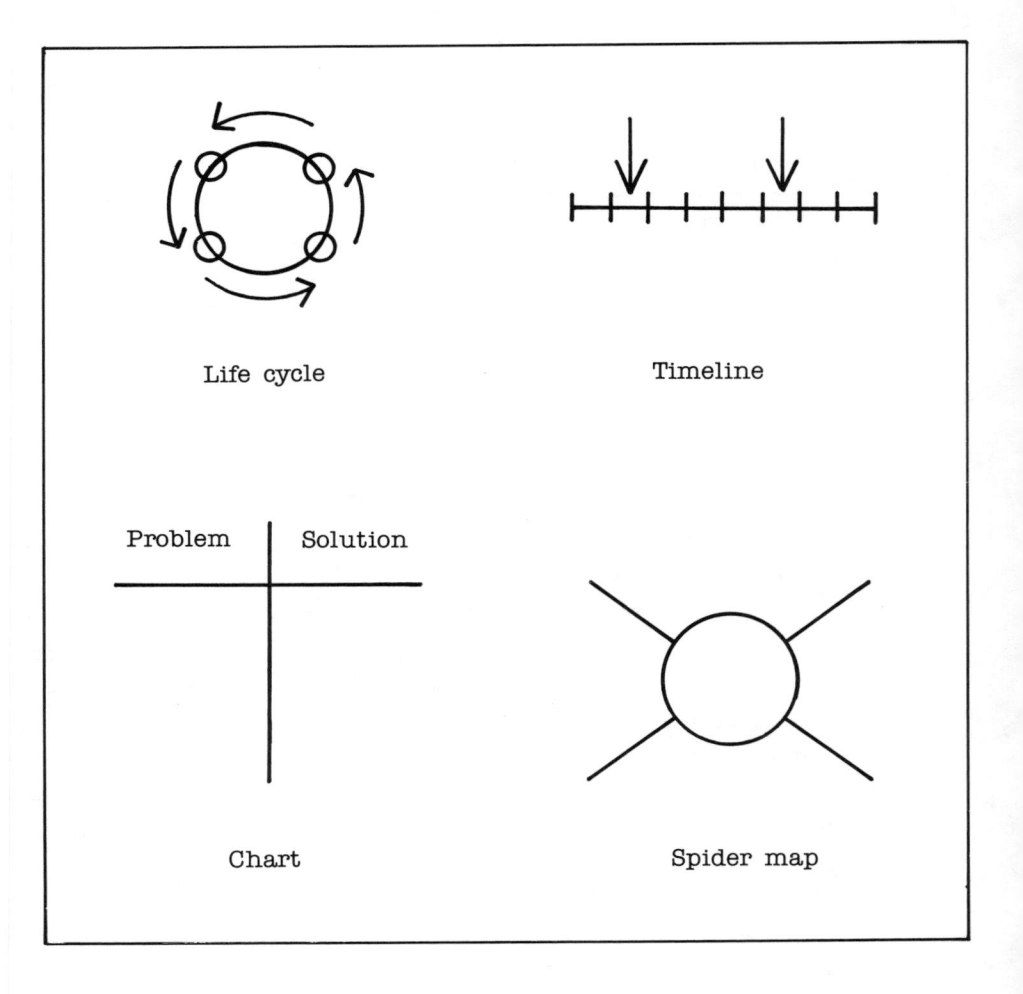

Life cycle

Timeline

Chart

Spider map

CONCEPTUAL WEBS*

Once all the words or phrases about a topic have been brainstormed the items or ideas can be linked.

Fresh
shrimp
prawns
Sea
cockles
trout
yabbies
salmon
crabs
lobster

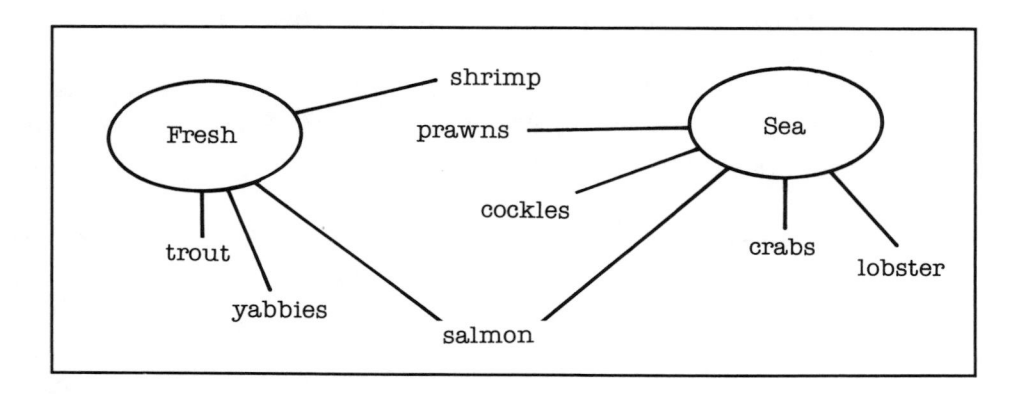

CLUSTERING*

When clustering, the word or topic is written in a circle in the centre of a chart. Lines or rays are drawn from the circle and main idea words are written on the lines. Branches with details are added to complete the cluster, for example:

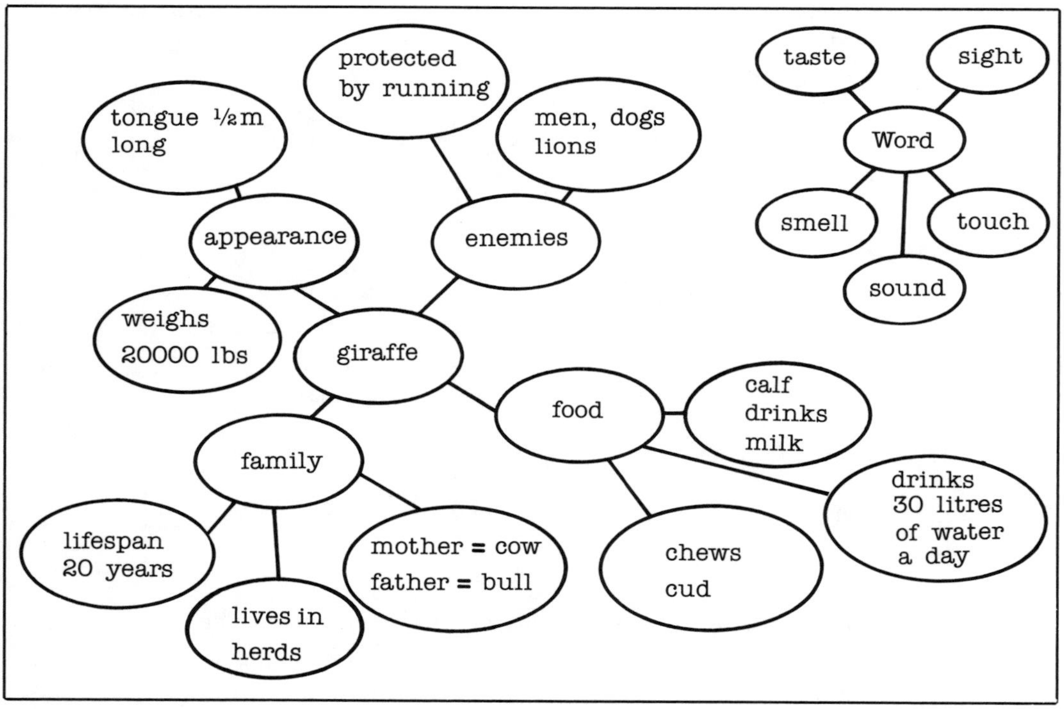

protected by running
tongue ½m long
men, dogs lions
appearance
enemies
weighs 20000 lbs
giraffe
food
calf drinks milk
family
drinks 30 litres of water a day
lifespan 20 years
mother = cow father = bull
chews cud
lives in herds
taste
sight
Word
smell
touch
sound

*Adapted from an idea in Haggard (1985).

Rather than have the whole group engage in mapping ideas we suggest that group members pair up and each pair develops its own diagrams from a brainstormed list. The whole group can then compare alternative ways that the information can be organised. Each pair can tell the class how the information was organised and why the choices were made.

In a Year 5 class children were asked, 'What is a family?'. After brainstorming all the ideas pairs worked together to organise the information. One pair represented the information as follows:

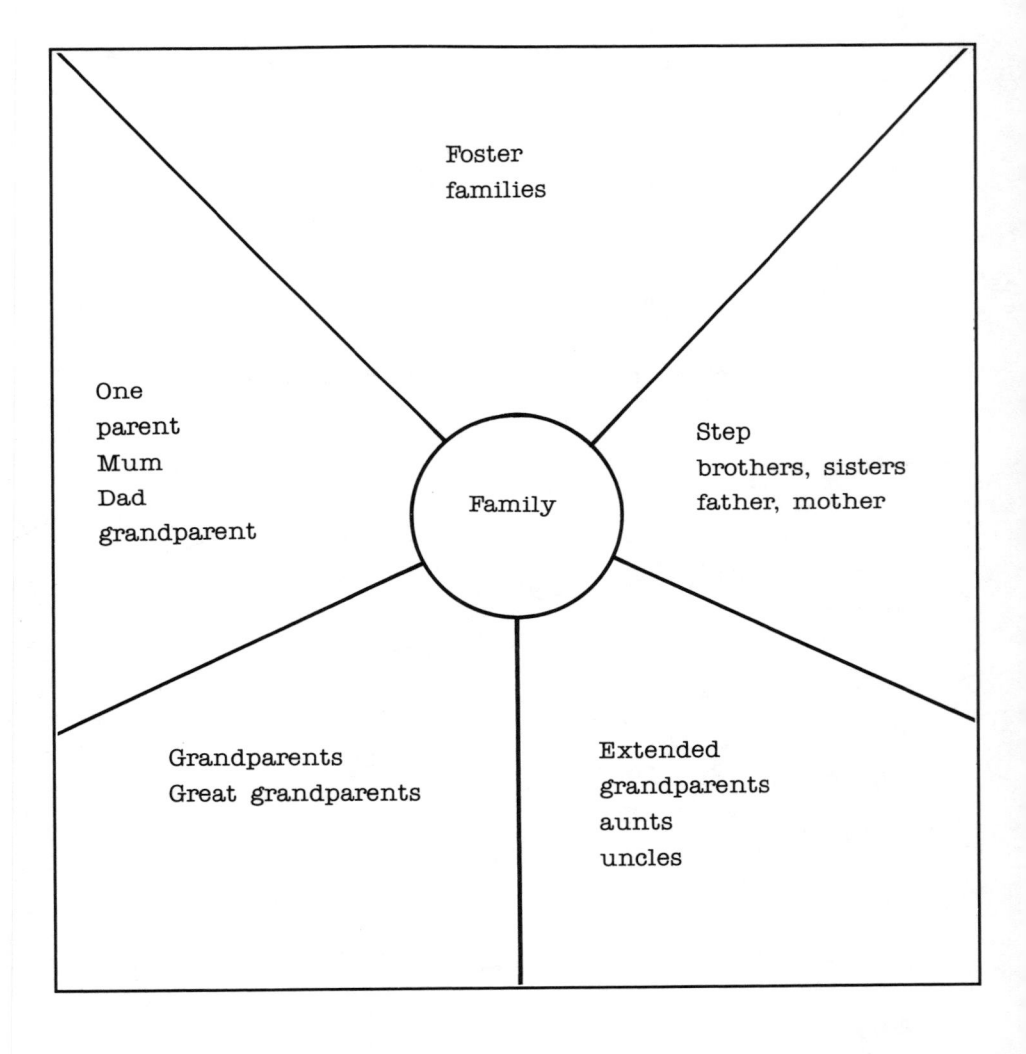

The same procedure for organising information can be used in a variety of situations. The information may be brainstormed or based on research from books, films, videos, class discussion or a combination of these. The topics are endless and may relate to any curriculum area such as reading, mathematics, social studies or science.

ACTIVITIES

PARTNER PROBLEM SOLVING

Once children have been introduced to the skills for solving problems these can be practised in pairs using issues that have arisen in class meetings or in the playground or elsewhere. The following suggestions are based on four steps for solving social problems outlined by Spivak and Shure (1974):

1. Defining the problem
2. Brainstorming alternative solutions
3. Thinking of consequences
4. Finding a solution

Begin with the class in a fishbowl circle. Introduce the four steps for problem solving to the class. Have the steps displayed for all to see. Next, set up a role play to demonstrate ways to find a solution to a problem. To make it easy the teacher could role play one part here to lead the discussion. The others in the class watch and provide feedback about how well the above four steps were followed.

For example, the pair could discuss a curriculum activity for reading like the one that follows on page 74. Any curriculum area where there

are choices for groups to work on would do. In this role play each member of the pair has a different preference for an activity.

Partners, after you have read the book *Space Demons* work together on a joint project.

You could:
- draw a mural
- make a readers theatre
- make a co-operative model of part of the story or
- write a response to the story to send to the author.

But each person wants to do a different activity so how do you choose a solution? Use these steps:

1. Defining the problem
2. Brainstorming alternative solutions
3. Thinking of consequences
4. Choosing a solution

1. Defining the problem

First the pair take turns to define the problem. They both want to do something different.

'I want to do a play because I know which part of the book would be easy to make into a script.'

'I want to do a mural and you need two people to work on something that big.'

'Well two people would be needed in the play too.'

The role players are asked to define the problem. This is an important first step to uncover the real issue or problem, which is:

'We have to work together as the activities are co-operative. More than one person is needed to complete the activities.'

2. Brainstorming alternative solutions

The second step is to ask children to brainstorm alternatives:

'Both work independently.'

'Both do a mural.'

'Both do the play.'

'Do something that both wouldn't like but it would be fair.'

'Forget the whole thing.'

'Do a play with a mural backing.'

'Think about it tomorrow.'

'I'll just do what I want.'

The goal here is for the children to come up with as many alternatives as possible. Good problem solvers are able to see a variety of solutions. At this point evaluations should not be made and solutions such as 'I'll just do what I want' should be accepted. The important point is for children to suggest a range of alternatives.

3. Thinking of consequences
At this step the children go back to the brainstormed list of the solutions and think of the consequences:

'If we don't work together it will take too long.'

'I can't draw but I can colour.'

'We would both need to be in the play.'

'If we don't co-operate we'll have to do something that won't be as interesting.'

This thinking of consequences is difficult at first for some. These children will need lots of practice.

4. Finding a solution
After defining the problem, coming up with an alternative solution and thinking through the consequences, the last step of finding a solution should follow quite easily. It is important to take time to go through this process slowly.

Feedback: This is provided by the observer and the class can then discuss how effectively the pair managed their differences using the four steps.

Practice: The class can break into pairs to practice using the skills. A different problem or topic is chosen.

Variation: Introduce a third person to the pair. This person asks questions to ensure that the four steps for managing differences are followed:

'What is the problem?'
'Let's brainstorm some solutions.'
'What would the consequences be of each of these solutions?'
'What can you agree on now?'

Once the steps for problem solving are made explicit, practised and feedback has been given, children begin to take responsibility for solving their own problems more and more, both in and outside the classroom. Topics to use for practising the skills for problem solving can easily be found in the playground.

GROUP PROBLEM SOLVING OVER FOUR LESSONS

Lesson objectives: To work together as a group to plan a town and examine how the buildings and services are interdependent.

Kinds of groups: Five children in a group, teacher assigned with mixed abilities.

Roles: The groups assign the roles of observer, summariser to speak for the group and a recorder. (An observation sheet example is shown on page 77.)

Materials: Each group has coloured pencils, marker pens and a large sheet of paper.

The lesson: The task for each group is written on the board.

Your group has the opportunity to plan a new town. There are to be three hundred houses. It is 300 kilometres to the nearest town and you are to decide on a plan for streets, location of houses, services e.g. telephone boxes, fire station, hospital, police station, child care centre, schools, shops and an entertainment centre. Your group should draw a map of the town. Select three people to act as a summariser, a recorder and an observer.

These problem-solving steps need to be taken:
1. Brainstorm ideas of what should be in the town.
2. Clarify ideas of what is needed.
3. Organise ideas by linking some services close together. (Keep this record.)
4. Work together on a draft plan.
5. Evaluate the plan. Check it against the requirements.
6. Develop a final plan.
7. Present the final plan to the class in lesson four.
8. Observers provide feedback to the group about the co-operative skills used in each lesson.

The observer can use this observation sheet:

Observation Sheet				
Name	Confirming	Clarifying	Criticising ideas not people	Seeing other's views

Observer's name ....
Group goal for the next group ....
....

JIGSAW

Jigsaw is a way of structuring the classroom learning so that groups work co-operatively on small parts of a problem. The groups later re-form and share ideas with the whole class. Jigsaw has positive interdependence built in as the smaller groups all fit together like pieces of a jigsaw puzzle.

STEP 1. DECIDE ON A TOPIC OF INTEREST
The topic could be broad, e.g. 'What is the greenhouse effect?', or for younger children, 'What lives in the sea?'.

STEP 2. GATHER RESOURCES

Resources on the topic could be magazines, books, people or newspaper articles. Ask children to bring resources from home, from libraries and from friends. Have the resources ready for the children to use at will.

STEP 3. BRAINSTORM ISSUES OR QUESTIONS

Take the topic the greenhouse effect and ask children to call out issues or questions about the topic. Appoint a recorder to record the ideas on a big newsprint chart.

Start with general questions and call for more specific questions as the brainstorm session develops. It is possible at the conclusion of the brainstorm, when ideas are exhausted, to ask children to vote for the five most interesting questions. As there will be some overlap in the questions brainstormed some will need to be deleted.

Some questions or issues could be:
- What is happening to the sea levels?
- What is happening to the vegetation?
- What affects the ozone layer?
- What can we do about it?
- What are governments doing?
- How does the ozone layer work?

It is important that all these questions are generated by the children. Teacher-imposed questions would not be as interesting for children to research.

STEP 4. ASSIGN EXPERT TEAMS

Groups of three, four or five children choose an issue or question to research. Each group is in fact to become a group with expert knowledge about its question. The time and depth of information will vary from class to class but at least two days can be set aside to find out the information. This information should be noted because at the end of the two days the expert groups break up.

Expert groups with three members

Re-formed into three co-operative groups

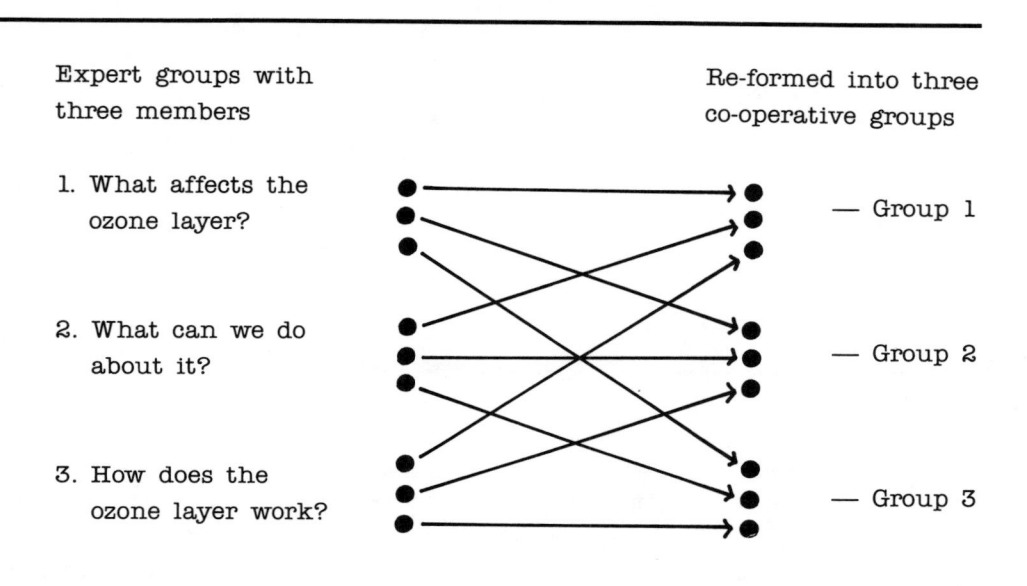

1. What affects the ozone layer?

— Group 1

2. What can we do about it?

— Group 2

3. How does the ozone layer work?

— Group 3

STEP 5. FORM NEW GROUPS

All experts re-form into another group of three, four or five. Each group member is an expert on particular questions. All the experts then tell other group members about the information they researched.

STEP 6. GROUP PROJECT

The groups with information from the different experts then commence a group project on the topic of the greenhouse effect. Ideas for group projects are open-ended and may involve:
• an advertising campaign to inform TV audiences
• letters to people with influence
• a board game to teach others about the issues
• poems
• songs
• reports
• stories.

◆

7

Managing Differences

United we stand, divided we fall.

◆

Differences of opinion, conflicting views and failing to reach consensus within groups of twenty or thirty people are inevitable. Furthermore, constructive conflict provides an important source of learning and should be encouraged. Within a cohesive and co-operative class any conflicts that do arise should be treated positively, as opportunities to teach children the skills for managing differences. Adults can give children the responsibility for solving their own problems instead of taking over and solving the problems for them. However, as with any co-operative skill, children will learn best if they are given lots of opportunities for practice.

The skills for co-operative problem solving discussed in the previous chapter encourage groups to explore alternative views before attempts are made to reach consensus. After brainstorming solutions and examining consequences a solution that suits all group members can usually be reached.

If the members of a group have difficulty finding a solution it helps to teach children how to state their position or view, look at the problem from another viewpoint, learn the skills of negotiation and mediation and finally, be aware of ways to reach consensus.

STATING POSITIONS

Stating positions is necessary to make sure group members or pairs understand each other's point of view. Students can use 'I want...', 'I think...' statements to prevent falling into negative accusing statements such as 'You did...', 'You are not...'.

SEEING ANOTHER VIEWPOINT

Try some different perspectives in order to see things from another's point of view. To help children see problems and solutions from alternative perspectives and to form a more considered consensus try the following activities.

Problem: How will we spend the $200 raised at the school fair? (or the problem could be how to plan a sports day or agree on a social studies topic.)

The class brainstorms ideas. There are three main viewpoints.

View 1   Spend the money on local homeless people.

View 2   Spend the money on Community Aid Abroad.

View 3   Spend the money on an end of year treat. We deserve it!

There are three viewpoints so divide the class into groups of six. (If there had been two main views, groups of four would have been organised.) Each pair will take one viewpoint and work out reasons why that view should be supported. (Time: approximately 30 minutes.)

1. Break the group into pairs and assign each pair one of the viewpoints.
2. Each pair works out arguments to defend its position. (3 minutes)
3. Each pair is then given time to present its arguments to the group of six. (6 minutes)
4. The groups discuss the three views and their supporting arguments after all views have been heard. (3 minutes)
5. Now each pair is assigned a different view. Steps 2-4 are repeated. (Allow about 6 minutes for working out arguments, presenting arguments and group discussion.)
6. Repeat so the last view is assigned to the final pair. (6 minutes)
7. Now drop the assigned roles and discuss the best solution. (6 minutes)
8. If consensus is not reached then a vote may be taken to decide on the best solution.

In this next activity children are encouraged to see a problem from several viewpoints as they try to find solutions to differences of opinion about playing football at school. Some footballers want to play football in the main playing space and other non-footballers say it should be banned because it takes too much space and is dangerous.

To manage the differences and solve the problem the following steps can be used most successfully.

1. GET THE IDEAS OUT

As a first step ask the children to explain the problem. Make sure that all the ideas are out in the open.

2. STEP INTO SOMEONE ELSE'S SHOES

1. Assign students to groups of four.
2. Assign points of view or perspectives to the pairs in the group of four. Two people take the view that football should be played and two that it shouldn't.
3. Pairs work out arguments to defend their position. They write down points if necessary.
4. Partners go back to their group of four and present their arguments.
5. After the arguments have been presented discussion between pairs can occur.
6. Now switch roles and argue for two minutes (at least) from the other point of view. To do this well the students would have had to listen well to the arguments put by the other pair.
7. Drop assumed roles and work on solutions and consequences in groups of four.

3. SOLUTIONS AND CONSEQUENCES

As a whole class brainstorm solutions and consequences. When all the solutions and consequences are exhausted a vote can be taken to decide on the best solution. For example:

Solution 1: Divide the oval in half

Consequences:
- Footballers wouldn't be able to play a full game because there would not be enough space.
- If the oval was divided everyone could play. Footballers could still play but in reduced space.
- A teacher would have to be on duty to make sure people didn't go over the middle line.

Solution 2: Two days a week football, two days other activities

Consequences:
- If lunch times vary in length there could be argument about who gets the longer times.
- The oval doesn't have to be split up.
- Everyone gets a fair go.
- There are five days in a week so someone would get two and the other three days.
- On the off days the footballers would have nothing to do so they'd get bored.
- The footballers could learn not to be narrow minded and learn a new game.

Solution 3: Football at recess, then have one day football, one day games during the lunch hour

Consequences:
- People could forget what day was what.
- Footballers are big and would just do what they wanted.
- Recess is too short to play a game of football.

Solution 4: Use the gym for football

Consequences:
- Rotate one day in gym, one day out, means all get a good deal.

4. REACH CONSENSUS

Agreement may be clear by this point but if not then each group may vote on a possible solution. Recommendation: Football one day, other sports the next day.

Feedback: As in all co-operative activities feedback on how the group worked is important. An observer can monitor the group's use of the co-operative problem-solving skills of confirming, clarifying, elaborating, criticising and reaching solutions.

NEGOTIATING

At times consensus cannot be reached without further negotiation. The conflict between differing opinions should be viewed positively as the presence of conflict provides an opportunity for children to become skilled negotiators. In a successful negotiation both sides should feel that co-operation has occurred and a WIN/WIN is felt by all. The steps for negotiating a solution to differences are:

1. State the position you take and say what is important for you.
2. Clarify/confirm the other person's position. If you don't understand the other person's position ask an open question for clarification, e.g. 'What do you mean by...?'. When you think you understand the other person's position then confirm this with a closed question, e.g. 'So you mean...?'.
3. Look for common ground. Explore the differences and find the common ground between the two positions. It is a good idea to map the differences by writing them down. In this way common ground or overlapping ideas can be found.

```
I think ........... > _____ Maybe I think _____
                     common ground
I think .......< _____ Maybe I think ....... _____
```

4. Look at alternative solutions and a whole new solution to the problem may arise. Brainstorming is useful at this point. The brainstormed ideas are not evaluated or judged but are listed as they come. Try to suggest as many solutions as possible.

5. Choose a solution. A WIN/WIN solution can be found when agreement suits both views. If agreement cannot be reached the group can choose to vote on the matter or call for an outsider to mediate.

MEDIATING

The steps a mediator takes are similar to the process for negotiating solutions. The mediator is most often the teacher, but there is no reason why children can't learn the process and act as mediators for each other.

The mediator's role should include the following points:
- Stay objective, don't take sides
- Clarify issues
- Ask both sides to use 'I' statements not 'you' statements
- Summarise both points of view
- Map the conflict and solutions
- Draw up a contract
- Give positive feedback to both sides where appropriate.

MEDIATION STEPS

1. GET THE IDEAS OUT

It is necessary to say that the mediator must not take anyone's side but is there to help work through problems. Ask both sides to describe the problem using 'I...' statements and not 'you...' statements which often attribute blame. 'I feel' is a good way to start as it focuses on the feelings and needs of the individuals.

2. CLARIFY THE ISSUES

Ask the students to expand on any ideas that are not clear. Summarise or rephrase these ideas to check clarity.

3. CREATE ALTERNATIVE SOLUTIONS

Ask each student to summarise the other's point of view. This helps the student to see another's perspective and allows the mediator to correct errors of understanding. Mapping the conflict by listing the conflict with its problems and solutions is useful for creating alternative solutions.

4. AGREE IN PRINCIPLE

Ask both partners if there is any point at all where both agree. It can be a very small point. Try to get both parties to agree to a small point as this is the place where further bargains or negotiations will occur: 'If Fred will...will you...?'.

Refine the negotiations so that a contract can be drawn up, if necessary.

5. DRAW UP A CONTRACT

Draw up a contract with both parties present. The contract must be achievable and behaviours clearly named and described. Have both parties sign. Contracts are not always necessary. Verbal agreements are quicker and easier but some children need clear, concrete reminders of decisions.

6. REVIEW AND REFLECT

Review the six steps that have been used so that both partners can use this process for managing conflicts without using the teacher as a mediator.

REACHING CONSENSUS

There are many ways to reach consensus:

1. Everyone agrees.
2. A majority vote.
3. Appoint a small subgroup to make a decision.
4. Accept the opinion of the person with the most expertise.
5. Ask the teacher to choose between acceptable alternatives.

Here are some activities to use to work through to lead to agreement on a solution.

DIAMOND RANKING

Nine statements (on small slips of paper) representing a spread of opinion are given to each pair. Each pair ranks the statements important, good, OK, not important or forget it by using a diamond formation.

```
          1
        2   2
      4   4   4
        7   7
          9
```

The most important idea is placed at the top of the diamond. The next two are in second equal position. The three across the middle are fourth equal. The next two are seventh equal. Once the pairs have ranked the statements they move to a group of four and try to reach agreement on the ranking of the same statements. The skills of negotiation are practised here.

NOMINAL GROUP TECHNIQUE

1. Start with a question or an issue, for example, 'How do we stop the accidents in the playground?'.
2. All write several answers on a sheet of paper. (5 minutes)
3. A recorder asks for all the ideas and writes them on a newsprint chart. (15 minutes)
4. Exhaust all the ideas and discard those that are similar.

5. Number the ideas.
6. Ask for clarification of each item but don't evaluate the ideas yet. (15 minutes)
7. Begin to search for consensus. Give each person five small index cards. Each participant then selects and writes on each individual card one of the five most important items for them. Next, decide on the order of preference and assign 5 to the idea of first preference, 4 to the second and so on. The cards are shuffled and handed to the recorder.
8. The results are tallied.
9. The top five ideas are recorded.
10. The group may vote on its first preference from the five ideas scoring the most points.

CLASS MEETINGS: PRACTICE FOR MANAGING DIFFERENCES

One of the best ways to learn about managing differences is the class meeting. The class meeting can be introduced to children as young as 5 or 6 years of age.

There are three different types of class meetings according to Glasser (1969): the social problem-solving meeting, the open-ended meeting and a curriculum issues meeting.

A LEARNING FORUM

As real issues and dilemmas provide the best context for learning how to solve problems and manage differences, the class meeting provides a useful and authentic learning forum. In a class meeting the children can decide on the items for the agenda, that is, items of real concern to them, their teacher and the community.

The roles of recorder, convener and observer can quickly be taught and prompt sheets for meeting procedures can support children as they use the meeting to bring problems forward for solution. As Betty Fox, principal of St Bernadette's, says:

'Class meetings can have many purposes but first of all they should be held regularly and the procedure for conducting the meeting should be standard. If the class meeting procedure or format is constant the children become familiar with the different roles of observer, recorder and meeting convener. The agenda items should not just be school problems like playground rules as this can lead to constant nit picking. The teacher can introduce the class to other items to discuss like local, state and world issues.'

CO-OPERATION

Class meetings work best when the class sits in a tight circle with the teacher seated as an equal member of the group. Assigning the roles of convener, recorder and observer plus expecting input from all members of the meeting sets up positive interdependence. There is a shared goal: to explore a problem and to solve it with recommendations for action. There is individual responsibility in that students contribute ideas and vote on particular issues. Finally the class meeting involves the whole class and contributes to class cohesion.

A CLASS MEETING IN ACTION

There are twenty-four children, eleven boys and thirteen girls, and their teacher. They hold their meetings in a spare classroom and they all sit on chairs in a circle. The convenor, the recorder and the observer sit behind a table arranged at one end of the circle.

The convener, recorder and observer have their names pulled from a hat to make sure that everyone has a turn at these roles. They wear cards naming the role they are to play. They follow a script of a meeting procedure. The agenda items are written on a small blackboard in the classroom and the items below were added during the week.

AGENDA
1. Wearing tank tops
2. Spending $100

If no items have been recorded on the agenda board and there is no business to finish from previous meetings then the class meeting should not be held. Class meetings are held when there are issues to discuss. Time limits should be set and adhered to. Setting aside time to report back on how people co-operated is very important.

The meeting begins.

Convener:	'Welcome to today's class meeting. This meeting will close in 30 minutes because it will be lunch then. Will the recorder read the decisions we made last meeting?'
Recorder:	'The decisions we made at the last meeting were to choose one person to help the Year Ones during lunch.'
Convener:	'Thank you. Are there any other items we need to add to the agenda before we begin?'
Mr Cameron:	'I would like your permission to add behaviour at the delicatessen as an item to follow up from our last meeting.'
Convener:	'The recorder will add that as the first item. Could we have some positive comments on how behaviour at the deli has improved?'
Mr Cameron:	'Mrs Franks said that the shoving has stopped so that's really good.'
Domi:	'David and Chris aren't yelling and pushing any more.'
Sue:	'The little kids said they aren't having their chips taken.'

Other comments are added.

Convener:	'The next item on the agenda is tank tops. Could you elaborate please, Mr Cameron?'
Mr Cameron:	'Well, it has been a school rule that tank tops and singlets aren't allowed to be worn during the summer months and the School Council is reviewing that rule next week. You could discuss this rule and make a recommendation and then I could take it to the School Council. I'm a staff member on that committee and I think your ideas on the issue need to be considered.'
Convener:	'Is there any discussion?'
Elliot:	'Will they also talk about thongs?'
Mr Cameron:	'I'm not sure.'
Grant:	'What about board shorts. Will they be banned?'

Other questions follow and the convener intervenes.

Convener:	'Instead of asking questions you should talk about whether tank tops should be allowed or not. You need to have arguments for and against tank tops and stick to the agenda item . . . Also there are people swinging their feet

	and disturbing others. Can you please stop this? Chris, what do you think?
Chris:	'I think that tank tops are really for the beach because they are casual and it's better to have casual clothes for weekends and school clothes for school.'
Jamie:	'I disagree. No one tells girls not to wear shoestring straps to school and they're as casual as tank tops. Both girls and boys should be able to wear what they like as there is no official school uniform that says everyone should wear the same clothes.'
David:	'Some people haven't got enough money to have two sets of clothes, one set for home and one for school.'
Convener:	'There are still people swinging their legs. What should I do about this?' (looks at Mr Cameron)
Mr Cameron:	'If it continues then the person can sit on the floor. There have been enough warnings.'

More arguments for and against tank tops are sought by the convener.

Convener:	'Time is nearly up. Are there any recommendations about tank tops?'
Domi:	'I recommend that tank tops stay banned at school.'
Craig:	'I recommend that it is a person's right to choose whatever they like to wear to school.'

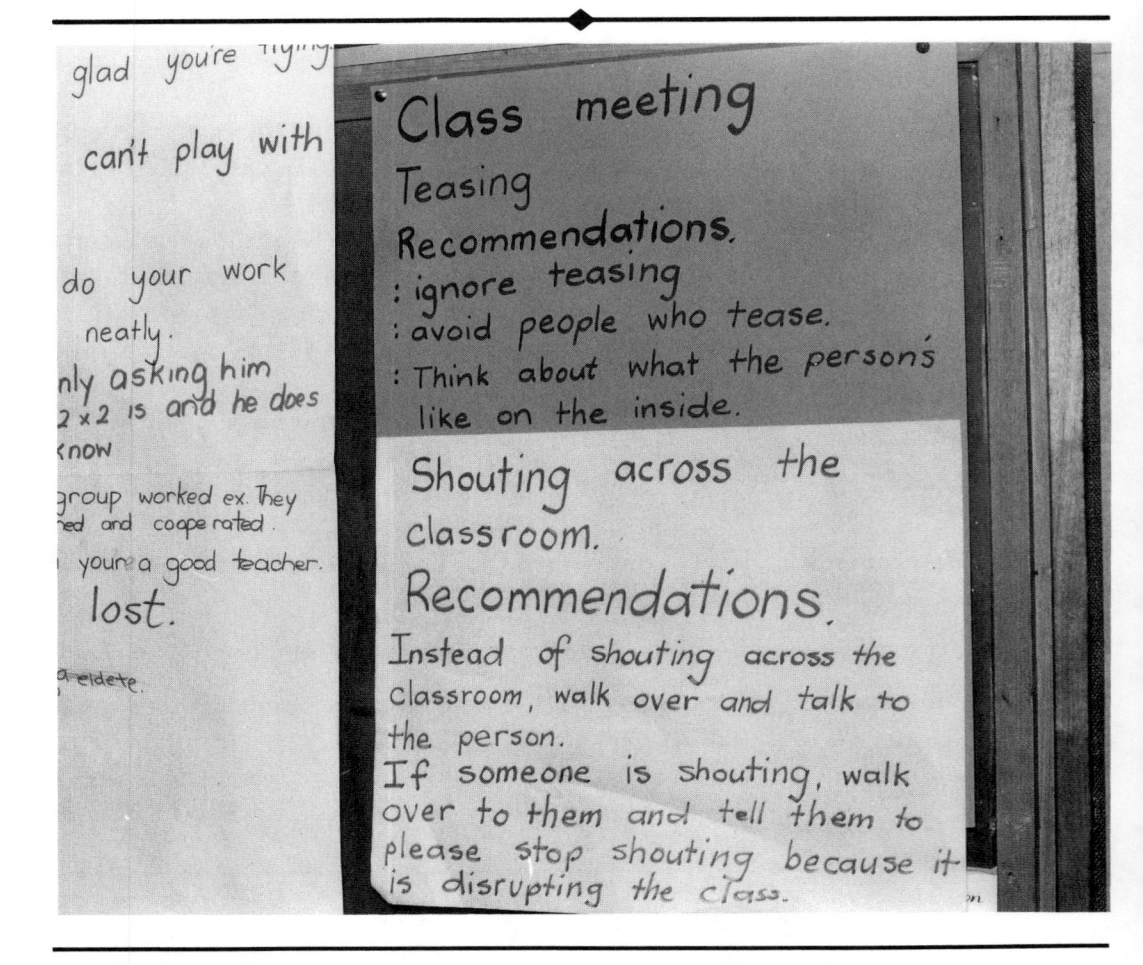

After several recommendations have been heard and recorded in the school meeting book by the recorder the children vote on which recommendation they favour. The observer counts the votes. The favoured recommendations have 'Passed' noted by them. The ones that do not have a majority vote have 'Not passed' noted against them.

Convener: 'The decision is that we recommend that tank tops can be worn at school.

'The next item on the agenda is spending $100. We discussed this last meeting and we will vote today. Will you read the recommendations from last time, recorder?'

As the meeting continues the recorder writes down the recommendations and number of votes. The observer watches for and records cooperative behaviour. At the close of the meeting the observer reports. This important step reinforces the need to continue to use co-operative skills and should not be skipped. It's better to cut short a meeting than miss the feedback and reflection time. If time is suddenly cut a quick 'whip around' the group with six or so children reporting on co-operative skills will do.

Convener: 'Can we have the observer's report please?'

Observer: 'Two people asked questions. Two people chatted to each other. Five people spoke clearly. Lots of people encouraged others to speak and fifteen different people spoke at the meeting. There were three put-downs. People all remembered to raise their arms when they wanted to speak.'

What do children say about class meetings?

Positives

- They help work out problems.
- Before class meeting problems used to hang around.
- It saves extra trouble for the teacher.
- Lets us make our own decisions.
- Helps us think for ourselves.
- Helps us run meetings.
- We learn to be organised.
- We learn to take charge of situations.
- Makes school a better place to be.
- Our class works better together.

Negatives

- Not everyone listens.
- Some decisions don't suit everybody.
- Some items that appear on the agenda are petty.

The various roles played in a meeting can be displayed in the classroom or in a meeting book*:

Convener's role

- Watch the time. You only have 30 minutes.
- Make eye contact with each speaker.
- If you get stuck or bogged down, move on and come back to it later.
- Don't give turns only to your friends. Be fair.
- Keep people on task. If they wander off the issue ask them if their comment is valid.
- If more information is needed ask people to elaborate.
- If a person's input is unclear ask them to clarify.
- Make sure that only one person speaks at a time.
- Be encouraging — support ideas.
- Try to summarise the discussion before any recommendations are made.
- If everyone votes for a recommendation it is called a unanimous decision.

---

* The following class meeting roles are based on meetings held at the Seaton Park Primary School.

Convener's script

1. Welcome to today's class meeting.
2. The decisions we made at the last class meeting were......... .
....
3. The first item on the agenda is ....from ....
   Could you elaborate please?
4. Any discussion?
5. Any recommendations?
6. We will now make a decision. Who votes for the recommendation
   that .... ?
7. The decision is ....
8. The next item on the agenda is ....from ....
   Repeat Steps 4–7.
9. The class meeting is now closed. Can we have the observer's
   report please?
10. Thank you.

Observer's role

1. Write in the observer's book:
   • the date
   • your name
2. Observe the class meeting for:
   • one person speaks at a time
   • eye contact
   • building on other people's ideas
   • people contributing to the discussion
   • summarising
   • criticising ideas, not people
   • put-downs
   • noise level
   • keeping on the task
   • voting
3. When you give your report remember to:
   • give positive feedback
   • not mention names
   • suggest ways we can become better group members
   • make eye contact with the whole group

Recorder's role

Write:

- the date
- your name

Read:

- the decisions made at the previous class meeting

Record:

- the items on the agenda
- the name of the person who wrote the agenda

Item:

- the recommendations
- voting results next to each recommendation
- highlight decisions made

Remember to write as quickly, correctly and as neatly as you can.

QUESTIONS ABOUT CLASS MEETINGS

What if agenda items seem petty?
Children need guidance in putting up agenda items that really need to be discussed. It is easy to waste time talking around issues where nothing gets resolved. Keep a time limit in mind.

What if the agenda items cannot be solved by the class?
Some issues, such as changing the speed limit on country roads, can present difficult situations. The teacher has the power of veto and can ask that the item be deleted if the class cannot act and enforce its decision.

What if class meetings turn into gripe sessions?
Sometimes gripe sessions can occur where comments like 'Jack never listens to anyone' or 'Cathy took my idea' are common. These sessions can be stopped if the convener reminds people to stick to the issue or calls for arguments for or against an issue. Asking for recommendations is one way to move the meeting out of a gripe session.

   Another idea is to cut discussion short and move on to the next item on the agenda. Finish the meeting early if the group really does not want to change or make a decision.

What if children see meetings as a waste of time?
Make sure the recommendations are acted upon. Meetings should not

be superficial activities. Many schools have a Student Representative Council with a nominee from each class who takes the class recommendations to the SRC and then further, to the School Council.

What if parents or other teachers see meetings as a waste of time?
Point out the reduction of behaviour problems, the oral language benefits of speaking to a large group on areas of real concern to the class, the attentive listening skills required to respond in meetings and the benefits of learning meeting procedures, which are so important in adult decision making.

What if disruptive behaviour occurs at the class meeting?
Put disruptive behaviour on the agenda for the next class meeting. All can discuss this and come up with recommendations. Talk about the behaviour in general and don't put down one or two children. Remember to have a feedback session on co-operative skills when the observer reports after each session.

What if the teacher always takes over?
Try not to next time. Count to ten. Ask the observer to count how many times the teacher speaks. If the teacher is judgemental and is set on finding fault and giving out punishment the meetings will fail. The teacher must remain non-judgemental and make sure the meeting is for problem solving as a group, not a sneaky way to undermine children's confidence and power to make decisions.

Do class meetings always have to be about rules and disputes?
There are social problem-solving meetings, open-ended meetings and curriculum meetings. The social problem-solving meeting is a forum for discussing behaviour, rules, and issues concerning the class and the school community. Open-ended meetings are where issues such as how will we spend the $200 we have raised for charity are discussed and a consensus reached. Curriculum meetings are useful for opening discussion to find what children know or have learned. If for example the children had studied a unit on world food production a meeting could be held to discuss the question, 'Do countries have trade tariffs on food? If so, why?' This would provide information to the teacher about the children's understanding of world trade and food production.

Should children and the teacher just sit anywhere?
The teacher sits in the circle and sits in a different place each meeting. Ideally the group should be mixed up so that there are no divisions according to race, class and sex. Glasser (1969) suggests that the teacher 'makes a systematic effort to arrange children so that the meeting will

be most productive'. Children who squirm and nudge one another can be separated. Boys and girls are interspersed, as are the vocal and quiet children.

When should class meetings be held?

Time should be set aside each week for a regular meeting and held if there is an agenda. The meetings are best held in the mornings just before recess or lunch as these times provide a natural cut-off point and keep the meetings short and to the point. Some teachers hold class meetings at times when children get tired or lose concentration. They find that a class meeting is so interesting to the children that their attention really picks up.

How long should they be?

As a general rule 30 minutes is best for junior primary and up to 45 minutes for upper primary.

What are the basic rules for class meetings?

1. One person speaks at a time.
2. Put-downs are not allowed.
3. All opinions are respected but different opinions are encouraged.
4. Emphasise 'I...' messages, not 'Some say...', 'They said...'.

8

WHEN DARREN WON'T CO-OPERATE

Focus on the problem, not the person.

◆

In most classrooms there are children who will not voluntarily join a group to complete a task. Some children might prefer to work alone; other children might join the group but then continually disrupt the group's activities. A teacher said of Darren:

> 'If Darren does any work with a group, five minutes later he's left the group and the group has broken up. He's not chosen by others to work in a group. He hasn't really got any co-operative skills. If he's playing a game with his peers he will have to run the show and have things his way. If he's playing cricket he'll have to bat more than anyone else or have control over the bat and ball somehow.'

Most of us will recognise children like Darren. They pop up in every class. One strategy for working with children like this is to provide them with a totally individualised program. This way the group can continue to work productively and children like Darren who have difficulty working in groups can at least get on with their own work. It might be argued that this strategy is the least disruptive to the class. Furthermore, the advisability of 'forcing' a child to work in groups when he might prefer to work alone could be questioned.

However, while separating Darren to work on his own may seem to work for a single lesson, in the long term this strategy may be self-defeating. It reinforces Darren's own view of himself and also the view of others in the class. It also denies Darren the sort of peer experience he needs most of all. Since social skills are learned Darren's behaviour indicates that he needs more practice at working co-operatively with peers, not less.

Research evidence suggests that children like Darren are very likely to suffer from feelings of loneliness. It also suggests that lack of social competence at 7 years of age is highly predictive of juvenile delinquency and school failure as an adolescent. (For reviews of research see Hill 1989, Burton 1987).

There are a number of reasons for the long-term nature of this problem:

1. Children who lack social skills generally have the least opportunity to learn these skills. They are more likely to work alone in the classroom and to have fewer opportunities for social interaction with peers.
2. Even when their behaviour does change, the reputations or attitudes that people have developed often make social acceptance by peers difficult.
3. Experience of social isolation and rejection lead to the development of a negative self-image.

Low self-esteem and negative self-image then can become further factors that make change more difficult. Children learn to take their low level of social acceptance for granted. Thus they become caught in a vicious circle of limited experience, poor reputation and low self-image. Rather than inadvertently contributing to this by always isolating such children from their peers, we can intervene in three ways:

Experience:	Provide children with positive social experiences with peers. These children need more opportunities than others to learn social skills.
Reputation:	Promote a cohesive classroom with positive attitudes from others.
Self-acceptance:	Provide experiences which allow encouragement and positive self-acceptance.

In general the strategies for teaching social skills to Darren are the same as those for other children. He needs to be aware of the required skills and he also needs practice and feedback. However, we need to take care that:

1. The child's experiences are organised so that they are not too threatening or demanding. The child should experience success.
2. The responsibility for participation rests partly with the individual and partly with the group. It is important that the group take on the responsibility of including all its members in whatever has to be done.
3. The child is not left out or does not always end up in the same group activities. This is very likely to happen if children are always left to form their own groups. Often the less socially adept children are put into a group with other children who lack social skills. There are definite benefits in selecting groups that include different levels of social competence.

The extent to which a teacher can achieve these things successfully depends largely on the classroom climate and cohesiveness. Cohesiveness directly influences children's dispositions to want to work co-operatively.

STRATEGIES

1. Develop a cohesive classroom that encourages a sense of trust and a feeling of belonging to a group. See the suggestions on pages 12–13.
2. Have a whole class discussion about tolerance. Everybody in the class can try to mention something about themselves that is hard to tolerate. This shows socially isolated children that behaviour problems are not confined to them.
3. The skill of 'including others' should be discussed by the whole group. The children can be asked to brainstorm specific things they can do and say to include others.
4. Use stories like *Piggybook* by Anthony Browne to demonstrate how co-operation is essential if everyone is to live together in families and work together at school. Books like *Alfie Lends a Hand* by Shirley Hughes provide strategies that children can use themselves to gain acceptance and entry into a group.
5. Use co-operative games as these provide a non-threatening context in which social skills can be practised by the whole class. There are some games that focus specifically on the skill of including others like non-elimination musical chairs, for example. (See Appendix 1, page 115.)
6. Children who need to practise social skills benefit from plenty of experience working in pairs or groups of three. Ideally pair a child like Darren with a socially competent child who will provide a good model. Working in pairs is less demanding than working in a larger group.
7. Playing the role of observer in a co-operative group activity provides a child with an opportunity to observe others without demanding active participation. Having to observe the positive social behaviour of others and then provide feedback is an important learning experience.
8. Role play activities can be useful. The key to maximising the effectiveness of role plays is the discussion afterwards. After children act out a theme then it should be discussed with questions like, 'What would you do in this situation if it were you?' or 'How would your father respond if you...?'

   Role plays can include situations like these:
   - Being the new person in the group
   - Being made fun of
   - Being rejected
   - Everyone talking at once and not listening
   - Being a teacher with a class that doesn't listen

- Hurting someone's feelings
- Making someone happy
- Communicating with someone who cannot speak English.

9. Discuss the problem of behaviour at the class meeting.

USING THE CLASS MEETING

Some of us may object to discussing an individual's problem behaviour with the whole class. However, social behaviours cannot be viewed simply as something that resides within individuals; they are concerned with relating to others. Social behaviours concern a group of people and can only be dealt with effectively by working with the group. The benefits of getting together as a group, in this case at a class meeting, and using difficulties as an area to understand rather than ridicule or scorn, far outweigh any possible harm to Darren.

As mentioned in Chapter 7 the raison d'être of the class meeting is not fault finding, moralising, judging or preaching but finding a solution to a problem. By asking the question, 'What can we do to solve this problem?', class members are caught up in thinking of ways they can help Darren be included positively in classroom activities.

When class meetings are used to solve social problems from within the class it is important that:

1. The problem is clarified first and all class members are encouraged to participate.
2. Factors which are presently blocking a solution to the problem are listed.
3. Group members identify the steps they can take to eliminate the blocks.
4. Those involved should make a commitment about the specific action they will take. (This is most important.) This might involve writing out a contract and obtaining signatures as a sign of commitment.

9

ASSESSMENT

All for one, one for all.
— Dumas

◆

Within a collaborative classroom, assessment is based on a democratic relationship between the teacher and students and assessment procedures differ from those of competitive learning environments.

In competitive situations the assessment focuses almost entirely upon curriculum content. In the co-operative classroom the assessment of children's co-operative skills and their knowledge of curriculum are equally important.

Within a collaborative classroom it would be inappropriate to have students compete for a small number of A's and B's while providing lots of C's and D's for most of the others. A competitive grading system, hierarchically controlled by the teacher, with students ranked against each other could be counterproductive.

In a democratic classroom the teacher actively seeks ways to encourage peer and self-assessment. The teacher and child jointly monitor the child's progress throughout the year, although assessment can also be periodic, after set units of work, or spontaneous and incidental.

In co-operative classrooms there is a continuing emphasis on feedback as children reflect daily on their progress. Asking students for oral feedback about what they have learned and how they learned is very revealing. Oral assessment is efficient and provides insights into the students' strategies and knowledge of the various curriculum areas and understanding of co-operative skills.

Oral feedback provides immediate information to the student to modify behaviour. Asking students to reflect on what they have learned and how they learned helps us to remind them that they are responsible for their own learning. Learners know best about what they have learned and how they did it. This leads gradually to students setting their own goals for future learning.

ASSESSMENT OPTIONS

GOAL-BASED ASSESSMENT

Goal-based assessment fits well into a democratic framework where there is careful negotiation between students and teachers. As students learn to take greater responsibility for setting their own goals greater motivation to achieve the goals is created. This contrasts with situations where the teacher imposes goals. The criteria for assessment are made explicit and carefully framed to allow for negotiation and choice on the part of the student.

Goal-based assessment can operate with goals set for a whole year, a term or a small unit of work. To begin the teacher specifies her overall goals for the unit. These goals relate to both social skills and curriculum content and are sufficiently broad to allow for student choice.

In setting goals for *social skills*, the teacher can explain the broad goals:

'This term my goal is to help you learn how to work as a group. We will practise leadership roles in all the language arts areas. The leadership roles are observer, summariser, clarifier, organiser, encourager and time-keeper.'

The children select personal goals they will work towards:

'I will be a good group encourager.'
'I will use lots of build-ups.'

Once the broad class goals are set children can select their own specific goals by referring to the list of co-operative skills for working as a group. Here, goal setting is carefully guided and yet personal choice is evident. Goals are recorded in a personal record file and once they are achieved they can be checked off. Goals for forming a group, working as a group, problem solving and managing differences can be recorded as the year progresses.

The same process for goal setting applies to *curriculum content*. The teacher has clearly stated broad goals and the children specify what goals they want to work towards.

Assessment can be ongoing or continuous throughout the school year. At times periodic or quick incidental assessment can take place.

CONTINUOUS ASSESSMENT

LEARNING PROFILE

A folder can be used to create a learning profile where children's social and curriculum achievements can be stored. This folder contains group products and individual products, such as samples of writing or lists of books read, with evaluative comments.

Lists of class goals and the personal goals of children can be checked off and stored in the learning profile once they are achieved. Group and individual observation sheets about how the group worked can also be kept here.

Some children use the front cover of the folder to record:

Nathan My Achievements	My Goals
enourager helping people predicting contributing accepting all ideas a worker not to put down	be a better recorder to summarize better speak better to be a better organize give others confidenc

PERIODIC ASSESSMENT

Specific skills may require assessment and group or individual projects can be devised where these skills are used and assessed. For example to assess several skills a research project could be carried out in a group. The skills of note-taking, organising information, summarising ideas and writing to include interesting information for peers could be negotiated and clarified by the group.

The co-operative skills for working as a group could be monitored by the teacher. The following skills could be agreed upon for assessment:

Group Project: Group Assessment			
	1	2	3 comments
Note-taking			
Summarising			
Organisation of topics			
Neat writing			
Effective layout			
Illustrations			
	** *** *** *** *** *** *** ***		
Group organisation			
Time-keeping			
Encouragement			

1 = excellent
2 = good
3 = needs more work (specify where)

The criteria for a 1, 2 or 3 are carefully negotiated so children have the skills made explicit, for example:

Note-taking 1 = • notes main ideas
• frames questions/finds answers
• details are under main ideas
• rearranged under major headings
• in point form
2 = • notes contain some main ideas
• frames questions/finds answers
• are in note form
3 = • needs work in main ideas/details
• find out how to ask questions of a text so that answers can be found
• needs work in noting using points

A group assessment of all the projects developed by the different groups, with comments for each of the above criteria, provides useful information to students about where future development is needed.

INCIDENTAL ASSESSMENT

Quick incidental and spontaneous feedback can be useful for assessing what children understand from the content or what children's attitudes are to a particular learning experience. The following ideas may be useful.

ONE-WORD CIRCLE

At the end of a session students form a circle and give a one-word summary of their feelings about the activity.

TELEGRAMS

Telegrams are short, sharp and to the point. A telegram of say forty words can be written to tell a group or the teacher how a session went. The telegrams can be dated and signed and may be posted in a postbox in the classroom. At times the teacher may want to reply to comments received if suggestions demand an answer.

Nov. 21.

We kept hands and feet to ourselves and told people there doing well. We didn't tease other people and put them down. We recorded what the people said so we can keep track of what people are saying

MOOD MESSAGES

The class stands in a circle and one by one tell how they feel by referring to the weather, an animal or food. The feelings are shared through analogy, for example:

'I thought the session made me feel like a seagull landing in the middle of a football match.'

'I felt like I was about to eat a chocolate sundae.'

'The session made me feel like a racing kangaroo.'

WHIP TECHNIQUE

The teacher asks a specific question like 'How were ideas clarified in the group?' and each person in the group quickly gives a reply. The reply is to answer the question so no other red herrings or issues off the topic are to be discussed. The reply should last 30 seconds at the most, hence the name 'whip'.

QUICK QUESTIONNAIRES

A format for a questionnaire can be developed so that there is space for skills to be added. The students can write the name of the skill and quickly record if the skill was used and by whom.

RECORD KEEPING
STUDENTS' RECORDS

To record progress that may be slow yet must be carefully acknowledged, simple recording procedures for daily or weekly achievements can be kept.

DAILY RECORDS

Some children need to refer to specific daily goals. The goals can be set up by the student after negotiating with the teacher.

Name ....

My goal today is .... (walk quietly, keep my hands to myself etc). Each time I remember to do this I will colour a cricket bat. Each time I forget I will colour the balls.

I remembered _____ times.   I forgot _____ times.

WEEKLY GOALS

Some co-operative skills take lots of practice. Describing the skills and having children monitor their achievement is a good incentive.

My weekly goals   Name ....

1.
2.
3.
4.
5.
Next week I will ....

POSITIVE RECORDS OF SUCCESS

If children record their achievements rather than their errors they can focus on what they do well rather than the demerits. In maths, for example, they can record how many were correct, rather than how many wrong:

1	2	3	4	5	6	7	8	9	10

They can colour the number of words they spelled correctly:

1	2	3	4	5	6	7	8	9	10

or record the number of books read:

Reading Log

Author	Title	start	finish
R. Klien	Dear Robin	13th April	30th May
P. Jennings	Unbelievable	10th April	1st May
C. Ransom	Thirteen at last	1st April	27th April
C. Ransom	Fourteen and Holding	13th April	5th May
M. Stewart	Love From Greg	10th May	15th May
M. Stewart	Dear Emily	15th May	15th May
I. Serrailer	The Silver Sword	15th May	22nd May
C. Thiel	Jodies Jorny	30th May	2nd June
C. Ransom	Fureteen at last	2nd June	19th June
A. Faragura	Gorillas	8th June	8th June
Class 6.0	Imaganary Animals	8th June	8th June
S. Townsent	The Secret diary of Adrian Mole	22nd May	28th May
L. Lowry	Anastasia Krupnik	2nd June	4th June
L. Lowry	Anastasia Again	2nd June	2nd June
R. Klien	Hating Atison Ashley	8th June	10th Jene
R. Dahl	Fantastic Mr. Fox	8th June	4th June
L. Lowry	Anastasia, ask your Analyst	17/2/89	23/2/89
L. Lowry	Anastasia at your service	23/2/89	6/3/89
L. Lowry	Anastasia on her own	10th Mar	13 Mar
R. Klien	People might hear you	6th Mar	13 Mar
J. Marsden	'So much to tell you'	13th Mar	20th March
A. Martin	The truth about stacy	11th July	21st July
A. Martin	Little Miss Stonybrook and dawn	11th July	9th July
F. Pascal	Teachers Pet	21st July	23rd July
L. Gleeson	Eleanor/Elezebeth	1st August	August
P. Farmer	Charlote Sometimes	15th August	17th Aug
A. Martin	Mary Annes Bad Luck Mystery	17th Aug.	25th Aug
C. Ransom	Going On twelve	25th Aug.	

Make class spelling boxes or class dictionaries in big blank books, where all the words the children have learned are stored alphabetically. Words are added as more and more are learned.

TEACHER'S RECORDS

Brief records of children's behaviours can be noted on small index cards and filed in an index box arranged alphabetically under surnames. Observations can be recorded and the need for action noted. Dates allow a record of occurrence of behaviour.

ANECDOTAL RECORDS OF BEHAVIOUR

Brief anecdotal records about children's behaviour create a useful record for planning further teaching sessions. If, for example, Sam only uses voting to solve a group's problems a teacher may note this and teach or reteach brainstorming and listing problems and solutions as techniques that delay voting.

MINI-CASE STUDIES

The mini-case study can have a child or a particular skill as a focus, for example eliminating put-downs. The teacher could note down when the focus behaviour takes place in order to bring it to the children's attention.

Put-downs	Where	When	Who

Action taken:

PEER AND SELF-ASSESSMENT

Both peer and self-assessment play an important role. As so much of the work undertaken in a collaborative classroom is group work, at times a group assessment or score may be given. With a group score everyone in that group receives a particular mark.

To encourage self-assessment, opportunities for self-reflection can occur regularly. It helps if self-assessment and assessment by the teacher are compared and discussed. Children's views of their performance often differ from the views of the teacher.

In co-operative learning, peers are taught to observe and give feedback on each other's co-operative skills. In addition, students in pairs may assess each other's work and work together polishing and refining the product. When children work co-operatively in this way, peer assessment provides important learning opportunities.

Self-assessment can occur as children achieve goals they have set. It is wise to crosscheck students' views with those of the teacher. If both teacher and student use the same assessment form they can compare and discuss any differences.

Use a form like this and check viewpoints.

Skills	Attainment	Effort
Listening	1---2---3	1---2---3
Taking turns	1---2---3	1---2---3
Quiet voice	1---2---3	1---2---3
Encouraging	1---2---3	1---2---3
No put-downs	1---2---3	1---2---3

1 = excellent   2 = good   3 = poor

Feedback and reflection is stressed as the most important step in learning to work collaboratively. Using the observer, who watches and reports back on the group process, means the assessment about how well the group worked is built into the classroom day.

Observation forms cue observers in to specific skills to look for, such as:

Observation Sheet   Group No ....

Summarises

Questions

Encourages

Eliminates put-downs

Group goal for next time is...

When children are aware of what specific skills or criteria are being used for assessment and they are clear on what the skills mean, most group sessions are successful in achieving their goals. Planning goals for the next group session shows that assessment and planning for improvement are linked.

LEARNING CONTRACTS

When contracts are drawn up skills or requirements can be specified so that group assessment is possible. If children have a reading contract it could look like this:

GROUP ....

Contract for week..................Name..................Date..................

• Read a novel of your choice.

Title ....

• Talk about your book with your group.

• Answer one of the questions from the roulette wheel.

As a group plan a short project; a readers theatre; or a joint oral report on the book to share with the class.

ASSESSMENT

1. Write a group report on how well you worked.

2. Have the class comment on:

    • entertainment value

    • knowledge of the book.

The group can take turns to read the book if there is only one copy, but the contract works best if there are enough copies for each student.

SCHOOL REPORTS

Subject areas and academic learning have monopolised the school report card for many years. But taking account of what we now know about how people learn collaboratively and the kinds of skills needed to work this way, school reports that presently focus on curriculum areas such as reading, writing, spelling, maths, social studies and expressive arts might also begin to include the co-operative skills of starting groups, working as a group, problem solving and managing differences.

Under each major heading, say starting a group or working as a group, it is possible to list subheadings and assess, first, whether the child has knowledge, i.e. have the skills or processes been made explicit or is reteaching necessary? Next can the child use or apply the skill? Finally and most importantly can the child assess his own use of the skill, thereby leading to improvement?

In this way the teaching of skills and processes in the classroom is followed up in the assessment procedures:

1. Has the skill been made explicit?
2. Has the skill been applied and practised?
3. Has time for feedback and reflection been given?

Students and the teacher may use the same form to monitor progress and then discuss any variations in their assessments. This information may then be used in subsequent school reports.

	Has knowledge	Applies knowledge	Reflects on effectiveness
Assessment: Co-operative Skills			
Name ....Teacher			
Starting groups			
Makes space for others			
Takes turns			
Eliminates put-downs			
Forms partners/threesomes			
Makes eye contact			
One person speaks			
Working as a group			
Observing			
Summarising			
Encouraging			
Clarifying			
Recording			
Organising			
Problem solving			
Brainstorming			
Clarifying ideas			
Confirming ideas			
Elaborating ideas			
Seeing consequences			
Criticising ideas			
Organising information			
Finding solutions			
Managing differences			
Stating position			
Seeing the problem from another viewpoint			
Negotiating			
Mediating			
Reaching consensus			
Self-assessment			
Peer assessment			

Learning to co-operate is a long-term process. It does not magically appear. Taking the time to make the co-operative skills explicit, providing time for practice and giving feedback help build cohesive classrooms. Cohesive classrooms are fun to belong to. Both teaching and learning in a co-operative environment become fascinating as we consider ways to encourage ourselves and others to learn.

◆

APPENDIX 1:

CO-OPERATIVE WARM-UPS

AND GAMES

◆

There are lots of times when we feel like a laugh, or some fun. These activities are useful after everyone returns to school after a holiday break. They may be useful early in the year, when children are not well acquainted. In our experience, co-operative games are worthwhile as a regular part of the school week. Children enjoy them and they promote co-operative behaviour and cohesiveness in the class.

Co-operative warm-ups are quick 5-minute activities to focus on a co-operative skill or to help people get to know each other. Use them in the classroom in the transition times between lessons, before the bell goes or when a particular co-operative skill needs lots of practice. Co-operative games are fun activities where groups work together against some force, such as gravity, or complete a task in a set time. The co-operative games have been divided into easy, quick games and more complex learning games.

These co-operative activities can also be used for the following purposes:
• to include children who have been left out
• to practise sharing and taking turns
• to practise helping others and for gentle physical touching
• for talking nicely to others.

As all these activities are for practising the co-operative skills the same process for teaching co-operative skills can be used: make the co-operative skill explicit, practise the co-operative skills and give feedback and reflection.

If a game or partner activity is played make sure the children know the skill and then set aside time for feedback and reflection to ask, 'How did we co-operate to play this game?', 'How did people make spaces for each other?', 'How did you decide to take turns?'.

SELECTING GAMES AND ACTIVITIES

Look carefully at the games played in the classroom and outside. Many games are just good fun and useful for practising particular skills. But many are competitive as children are slowly eliminated until there is one winner and lots of losers. If we are working hard to establish trust, cohesiveness and co-operation in the classroom the games we play need some critical evaluation.

We have observed children playing the game *Circle Murder* where the children sit in a circle and one person, the murderer, winks secretly at people and thereby kills them. This looked like a good game for practising eye contact and non-verbal skills but closer examination reveals it is a game of elimination where eye contact is sought in order to trick a player. The game really encourages avoidance of eye contact. Another game that is used to practise attentive listening skills is *Simon Says* but again trickery and leading people astray are used to eliminate players until there is one winner.

Other competitive games to avoid are described by Cartledge and Milburn (1986):

Taunting/teasing games: Children are required to chant or call another player names, e.g. king of the castle, Mr Wolf.

Grabbing or snatching in scarcity situations: A situation is presented where there are more children than objects (chairs, beanbags) and children who can grab an object can stay in the game at the expense of others, e.g. musical chairs.

Monopolising or excluding other children: A situation is organised so that some children are in control (of a ball or a situation) and use their energy to keep other children from participating, e.g. keep away ball games and circle games where people are trapped inside or outside.

Physical force: Situations where children pull another across a line or hit another with a ball, e.g. brandy, piggy in the middle.

Find games that strengthen rather than minimise co-operative social skills. Many competitive games can be modified so that there are no winners and losers. For example, if players play against time, gravity or other physical forces or co-operate to solve problems they can all win and have fun. This shows the child who says, 'Someone's got to lose or it's no fun!', that fun is not just winning at the expense of others.

QUICK WARM-UPS

SITTING CIRCLE

Participants stand behind each other in a circle all holding the waist of the person in front of them. At a given signal from the teacher all bend knees and sit down on the person's knees directly behind them. For this to work people have to sit carefully and slowly. The circle has to be self-supporting. If it doesn't work first time make sure there is not too much distance between the participants. Also make sure that a proper circle has been formed.

When the circle is perfectly balanced ask participants to lift their left hand, then their right hand. If they can do this perhaps they could then try lifting their left leg. If the group has great solidarity they may take tiny little steps around the circle but still sitting on each other's knees.

Variation*

This can be played like non-elimination musical chairs. Children walk in a circle holding on to each other's waist. When the music stops all sit on each other's knees.

NON-ELIMINATION MUSICAL CHAIRS

The object of this game is to keep everybody involved even though the chairs are systematically removed. When a chair is removed and the music stops people have to help others sit down on the chairs somehow. This means sharing a chair or sitting on each other's lap. Eventually one chair is left and the whole group sits one on top of each other, holding on tight.

HUMAN SPRING

Children divide into pairs and stand about 2–4 feet apart facing each other. They hold palms at chest level and fall onto each other allowing hands to meet in the middle. They then bounce like a spring off each other and go back to the upright position. Now they fall towards each other again and bounce back from the other's palms. If partners get very proficient, they could try doing it balancing on one leg.

MIRROR REFLECTIONS

This can be done as a whole class or in pairs. The first person makes very slow actions with her hands and arms. Others follow the actions making a mirror image. If this is done very slowly it demands very careful observation to make sure that even the smallest finger movements are mirrored. Have 2–3 minutes for each image.

GROUP MACHINES

Work in groups of six to eight. Each group has to construct a machine with movable parts using all the members of the group. Body parts are used to create the machine and participants have only 5 minutes to cre-

ate, then rehearse the machine. After a short rehearsal the machines are shown to the class and all have to guess what they are.

SPIRAL

Participants form a large circle all holding hands. The teacher lets go of the person on her right hand. This person then starts walking around the back of the circle in a clockwise direction pulling all the other participants behind her. All participants, holding their neighbours' hands tightly, follow the person in front. The teacher, now last in line, holds her ground with feet apart for balance. Gradually a human spiral is created.

When the spiral is complete the teacher is encased by the class. She eases her way down and through the arms and legs of the people at the outer edges of the spiral, pulling other participants with her. If the teacher walks in a clockwise direction the complete circle can be re-formed with participants facing outwards.

Participants really have to help each other hold on to hands and they come in very close proximity to each other. (Not a hot day activity!)

WARMER...COLDER...

One player leaves the room while another player hides an object. The class then decide on what signals they will use to give clues to the absent player to find the object. They could clap, click fingers, hum loudly if the player gets closer to the object. When the player comes back into the room he or she is told what the clues will be.

GOING DOTTY

Students sit in a circle and close their eyes. The teacher places a different coloured self-adhesive dot on their forehead. (Use four different colours and have the same number of each colour.) Spread the dot colours amongst the students so that people with the same colour are spread out across the class. Students then open their eyes and, without speaking, try to form groups of the same coloured dots.

Students don't know what colour they have because their eyes have been closed.

Note: This activity shows how important non-verbal skills are in co-operation and how the whole group can help each other to solve problems quickly.

Variations*

1. Colours can be unevenly distributed with some groups having lots of members and others having one or two. Discussion of how individuals feel as majority or minority members can follow.
2. Rules for how the group can join up to make a circle can be given:
   • blue may join white or red
   • red may join green or yellow
   • green may join blue or red
   • white may join yellow or blue
   • yellow may join red or white.

CHINESE WHISPERS

A group of four children stand blindfolded at the front of the class. A class member whispers a message to one of the four. That person removes his blindfold and the blindfold of the next person in the line then mimes the message. Then person 3 takes the blindfold from person 2 and mimes the message. Person 2 copies the mime for person 1 who has just had her blindfold removed. Person 1 mimes the message for the class and they guess what the original message was. There should be time for lots of discussion about using non-verbal clues in communication amidst the laughter created in this activity.

Variation*

The class sits in a circle and passes a verbal whispered message from the first to last person. Discuss the importance of careful listening and speaking.

SET AND MATCH

Students are given pictures of objects, fruit, clothing or animals and have to move around the classroom to find people with pictures that match theirs or make a set. When they have found all the set members they sit down and try to invent a name for their set. Discuss how the sets were made. Did anyone feel part of two sets? How were decisions made about who belonged in what set?

CRAZY ANIMALS

Children make groups of four. One person has a piece of paper which is folded into four. The first player draws the head of an animal, folds the paper over so the head can't be seen then passes it on to the next person. This person draws the top of the body, the next person draws the middle and the last person draws the legs, bottom or tail or whatever. When the last section is completed open out the paper and see what has been drawn.

MR SQUIGGLE

Children sit in groups of four at a table. Set a time limit of 1 minute for each person to draw. One person begins by drawing a shape on the piece of paper and then passes it on to the next person who tries to make the shape into something. When the minute is up the paper is passed on. At the end of 4 minutes see what has been made.

MESSAGEMATCH

A piece of a message or a single word is given to each student. Students then walk around the room trying to match up other parts of the message so that it makes sense. Messagematch can be played in three stages.

1. One message is duplicated so that a single sentence is cut up and children fit words together to make a message.
2. Several messages are circulated and children have to find where their message best fits.
3. Students work in groups of four to six and devise their own messages of the same number of words as the number in the group. All groups jumble the messages and repeat as for stage 2. If start and finish are written on the appropriate cards it is easier.

CHAIN STORIES

One child begins a story with a sentence. The next person continues it by adding another sentence. This continues around the group.

GOOD LUCK, BAD LUCK STORIES

This is similar to chain stories except one person starts, 'What good luck I found a pot of gold.' The next person continues, 'What bad luck it had a hole in it.' The next person begins 'What good luck...' and so it continues.

LINE-UPS

There are several versions of this.

Height line-ups

Line up from shortest to tallest in a line or circle if there isn't very much space. Now the participants have to close their eyes to do this. (If you are really mean you can ask them to do this without talking. Non-verbal signals are invented in no time.)

Birthday line-ups

This line-up starts at January. Again this line-up is silent and nods, stamps and hand signals are used to communicate.

First name line-up

This is like the others but is usually done very quickly as people line up in alphabetical order.

1,2,3,4

To begin ask the participants to hop around the room on one foot. They then connect arms with two other people hopping on the same foot. Once a group of three has been formed play scissors, rock or paper, the game where you make those shapes with your fist.

Variations*

1. Have group members try to hold out the correct fingers to make eleven in total. There should be no talking.
2. Try to make twenty-three with two fists as tens and other fingers to make the three.

EASY CO-OPERATIVE GAMES

The following co-operative games are played for fun. Some of them fit into the warm-up section equally well but are included here because they are more complex than the quick warm-up activities.

BECAUSE

The first player describes an event, the second player gives a reason for the event and the third the probable effect of such an event, for example: 'We were late for school', 'because there was a great flood', 'and now we'll miss out on recess'.

CO-OPERATIVE NUMBERS OR SHAPES

In groups of three or four children use their bodies to make letters or numbers. All children must be included. Groups show each other the letter or number and the others guess it.

*These games are from various sources particularly Pike and Selby (1988) and Johnson and Johnson (1985).

BARNYARD

Participants stand in a circle with their eyes closed and number off. Animals such as pigs, ducks, sheep, cows, donkeys and chickens are assigned to the various numbers, e.g. 1 = pigs, 2 = cows and so on. Then with eyes closed the animals walk around 'baaaing' or 'clucking' until they find the others in their group. When others are found they join hands. At times teachers can number off people to mix different genders or outgoing and shy people.

BIG SNAKE

The children start by stretching out on their stomach and holding onto the legs of another person to make a two-person snake. This snake slithers across the floor to join up with another pair, then another pair until the whole class becomes a snake. The whole snake can turn over or curl up and this takes lots of co-operation.

FROZEN BEANBAG

The children move around the room with a beanbag on their head. At times they are asked to hop, to jump, to run, to walk. If the beanbag falls off players are frozen until someone picks up the beanbag for them. To pick up a beanbag your own beanbag must stay firmly on your head. At the end of the game people can describe how many times they helped someone or were helped themselves.

KNOTS

Everyone closes their eyes and walks around trying to take the hands of two other people. When everyone is linked up they all open their eyes and try to untangle themselves without dropping hands. The group must work together to untangle the knots.

WOOLLY WEAVE

Taking a ball of wool the first person wraps it around her waist, then passes it on to the next person who also wraps it around his waist. The wool is passed on until the whole class is wrapped up. The last player unwraps the class.

TOUCH BLUE

The leaders say, 'Everyone touch blue' or another colour or object. People all race to do this and try to touch something on another person. There are lots of versions of this such as, 'Touch a red shoe', 'Touch a ribbon', 'Touch a nose with your thumb.'

MAKE ME LAUGH

Participants are in a circle and each turns to the left and attempts to say or do something to make the other person laugh.

MORE COMPLEX CO-OPERATIVE GAMES

I'M COUNTING ON YOUR CO-OPERATION
For thirty students have thirty self-adhesive spots each with a different number from the chart below:

80	50	90	60	40	70	60	55	80	75
10	25	5	20	30	15	30	5	5	20
10	25	5	20	30	15	10	40	15	5

Students form a circle and close their eyes. A numbered dot is given to each person, then eyes are opened. (Try not to put numbers from the same vertical column on neighbouring students.) Students are asked to form groups of three without speaking. Each group's numbers must add up to one hundred. Students will form partnerships early only to find that they must break up the partnership in order for the whole group to form groups adding up to one hundred.

Variations

1. If the class number is less than thirty leave out columns, e.g. leave out two columns if there are twenty-four students. If there are students left over they can act as observers of co-operative skills and report back to the group on how they solved problems.*

2. With younger students the numbers can add up to ten. Groups of three can still be formed in the same way. Even smaller numbers can be used for the very young or special child.

WHAT AM I?

Sticky labels or cards are attached to people's backs. On these labels are printed, for example, the names of famous people, fruit, vegetables, or parts of the body. The whole group circulates asking questions that only get a yes/no answer from others in the group as they try to work out what the name or event is on their own back. Participants can ask only one question of a person without moving on to another player. When participants know who they are they still circulate, asking questions of other people. It is a good idea to step in and suggest questions that can be asked in order to prevent total frustration, for example, 'Why don't you ask me if I'm dead or alive?' or 'Why don't you ask me if I was a rock singer in the 60s?'.

Variation

The names on the back can vary with the age and interests of the participants. The name could be someone in the news — 'Am I a woman?', 'Am I in politics?' — and for younger children the name could be accompanied by a picture.

CO-OPERATIVE BUZZ

This is similar to traditional buzz where the whole group stands in a circle and numbers off after each other. If the rule is people sit down when a multiple of 7 is heard, instead of sitting down the children form another group. Set a time limit as the game goes on and on.

CO-OPERATIVE WORD SENTENCES OR EQUATIONS

Prepare a set of cards with a word written on each of them (the nouns could be red, the verbs blue and so on). Alternatively numbers and symbols for number operations can be recorded. Give out all the cards to the members of small groups of four to six, e.g. participants. Give Bob all the verbs, Sally all the adjectives and Barbara all the nouns.

Set different tasks such as make the funniest sentence, make the longest sentence, make a long equation or make as many equations as you can that equal ten. Share the groups' findings with the whole class.

CO-OPERATIVE CONCENTRATION

Prepare concentration cards that match, for example:

4	2 + 2

Who was Prime Minister of Australia in 1975?	Gough Whitlam

The players sit in a circle holding one or two cards that no one can see. One player begins by calling on a player to show a card, then another player is called in an attempt to make a match. If a match is made by group consensus the matching cards go into the centre. If the cards don't match they are concealed. The players on both sides of the person having her turn are designated as helpers. The game is won when all the cards are placed in the centre. The whole group wins.

Variation*

This game can be made easy or difficult. Simple shapes can be matched in pre-school. With older children devise cards where there are fine shades of meaning in cards that almost match. The role of helper ensures that most people are involved in the game.

PEACEFUL NEGOTIATIONS

Glue four different-coloured pieces of paper together into a square. Children are asked to form four groups of equal size. The minimum number in a group would be two. Each group is a country, represented by a colour, and has its own Foreign Minister and Road Builder who are elected by the group.

The object is for each country to build as many roads as possible from its own territory into the other countries. There are two conditions for building each road: (1) permission to build must be obtained from each country the road is to go through before construction takes place, and (2) if it is necessary to cross another country's road outside one's own territory, then permission in every case must be sought. All negotiations about permission are conducted through the Foreign Ministers.

Two things are not allowed: (1) building a road through the centre point where the four countries touch, and (2) allowing a road to fork so two roads are created.

All roads are drawn by the Road Builder in the colour of the assigned country. Other group members are citizens of the country and can discuss issues with the Foreign Minister. The teacher should explain the rules at least twice then leave the groups to work through the activity.

Variation*

Roles could be assigned to countries:

Power hungry: You think it's best to show your power continually to remind other smaller countries of your place in the world.

Protector: You are very powerful and see yourself as protecting the weaker countries.

Independent: You are a small country that wants to be independent but you have to join with a powerful country as the big powers are too strong.

Power player: You want to be independent. You are a small country who has to play the big countries off against each other because they want your friendship.

Other roles could be given such as political beliefs, scarce resources or rich resources and technical knowhow.

RESOURCES

The co-operative games described in this section of the book have been drawn from a number of sources. These included:

Pike, Graham & Selby, David 1988 *Global Teacher, Global Learner*, Hodder & Stoughton, London

Johnson, David W. & Johnson, Roger T. 1985 *Warm Ups, Grouping Strategies and Group Activities*, Interaction Book Co., Edina MN

Orlick, Terry 1978 *The Co-operative Sports and Games Book: Challenge without Competition*, Pantheon, New York

For sources of further co-operative games and activities see also:

Harrison, M. 1976 *For the fun of it: Selected Co-operative Games for Children and Adults*, Friends Pevre Committee (Nonviolence and Children Series) Philadelphia

Sobel, J. 1983 *Everybody Wins: Non-competitive Games for Young Children*, Walker & Co, New York

Orlick, Terry 1982 *The Second Co-operative Sports and Games Book*, Pantheon, New York

*Adapted from Pike and Selby (1988).

◆

APPENDIX 2:

ACTIVITIES FOR PAIRS
OR GROUPS OF THREE

_____◆_____

The activities that follow are suitable for age groups from 5 years to adult, although modifications will be necessary to suit various audiences. The discussion topics for the pairs and groups of three can be selected by the children or chosen to fit in with social studies, science or other curriculum areas currently being studied.

SELECTING PAIRS

We all communicate and co-operate quite easily when working with friends, but when people have to work, talk, listen and co-operate in groups with others, more sophisticated co-operative skills are needed. Assigning pairs of mixed ability, race, age and/or gender will encourage the more conscious use of co-operative skills and help create greater understanding. After all it is learning to communicate with lots of different people that will extend co-operative skills and provide real purpose to these activities.

NUMBERING OFF

There are many ways to ensure a mix of gender, age and ability. Random selection shows children you are not deliberately engineering groups of people to work together.

1. The teacher designates the pairs by numbering off 1&2, 1&2, 1&2, 1&2 etc.
2. Number off the whole group from 1 to 30. Add 1 to the final number (in this case 31). Now ask children to form a partner with someone whose number can be combined with theirs to make 31, for example 1 goes with 30, 2 goes with 29 and so on.

3. Number off 1, 2, 3; 1, 2, 3; 1, 2, 3 etc. All the 1s go together, all the 2s go together, and similarly the 3s.
4. Give all the boys a number from 1–10. Then give the girls a number 1–10. Children then find partners with the same number.
5. Put two sets of numbers 1–15 in a hat. Children draw out a number and form a pair with their matching number.

MOVING FROM PAIRS TO LARGER GROUPS

PAIRS WORK TOGETHER
In pairs, children can be given the task of finding which five foods they would take on a picnic. Both must agree on the five foods. Provide paper and pencils so that ideas can be brainstormed then deleted if both people don't agree.

PAIRS JOIN OTHER PAIRS
Pairs can be joined by another pair to reach consensus on which five foods to take on a picnic. The group brainstorms ideas then deletes those that not all group members agree with. It helps if a group recorder and a group reporter are assigned. A group reporter can then report the group's decision to the class.

PAIRS BECOME TRIADS
Another way to extend from pairs is to move to triads where the pair is observed by a third group member. The third member is an observer and gives feedback to the group on its use of co-operative skills.

LARGER GROUPS TAKE ON GROUP ROLES
Once groups of three or four are formed the role of recorder, reporter, encourager and observer can be assigned by the group members. Now everyone in the group has a part to play. To make sure children know what is involved in playing these roles the ideas for making co-operative skills explicit can be used.

TAKING TURNS

MAGIC MICROPHONE
Make a microphone shape or decorate a paper towel roll and introduce this as the magic microphone. The person holding the magic microphone can speak; when the microphone is not held, children are silent. When a person has finished speaking the microphone goes on the floor or table between the speakers.

The magic microphone encourages shy children to speak as the listeners focus more on the microphone and this takes some of the pressure off the speaker. If children have nothing to say they cannot be forced to speak. The microphone is merely a support for them. If children are in pairs or threes, a microphone will be needed for each group.

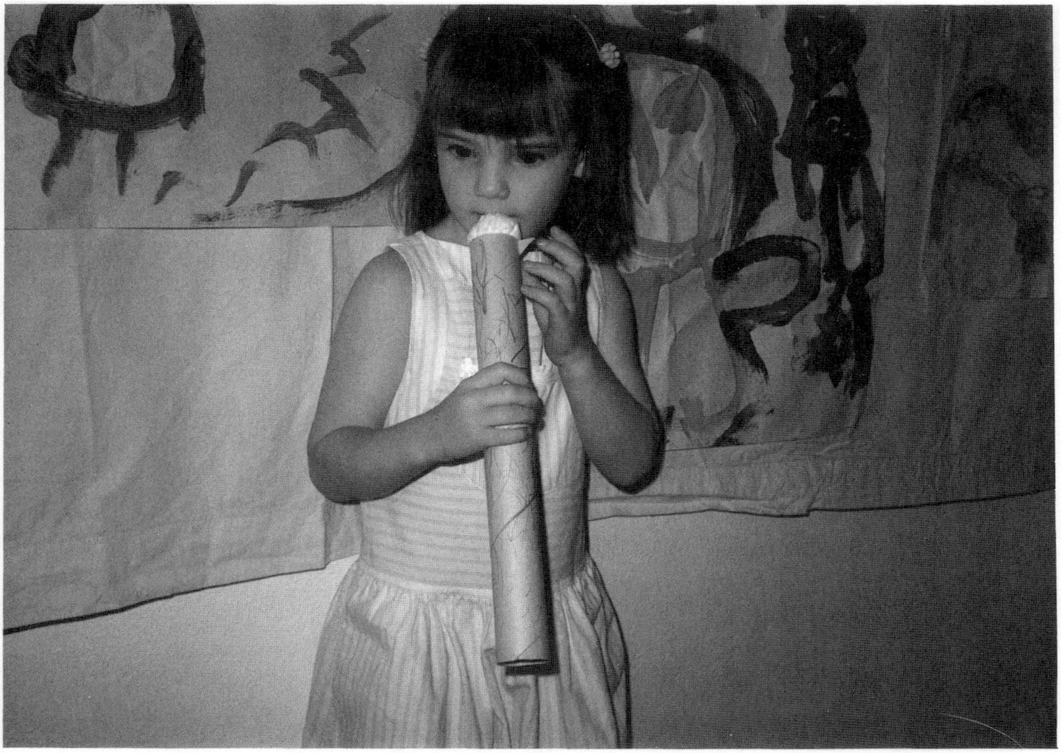

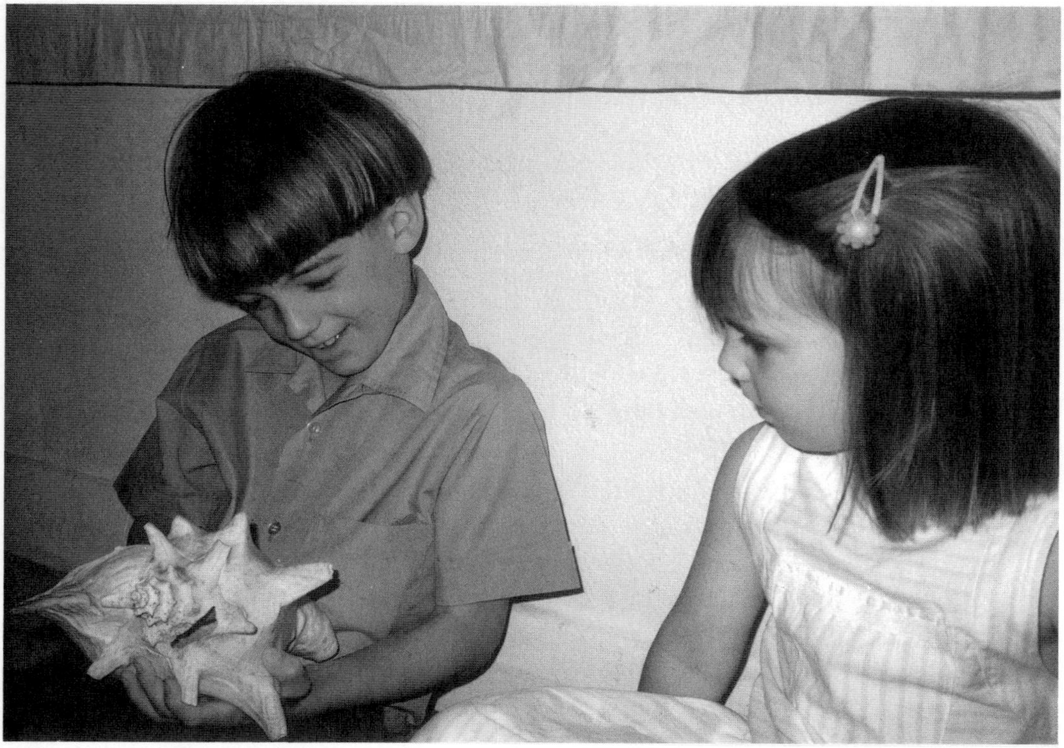

CONCH DISCUSSIONS

This is similar to the magic microphone except a real shell is used. Older children can be told a shortened version of the story *Lord of the Flies*. (In the book Ralph, the leader, tried to make sure that people had a chance to speak by using a conch shell placed in the centre of a group.) When someone wants to speak they pick up the shell. When they have finished speaking the shell is returned to the centre. Returning the shell to the centre gives people time to reflect on what they want to say.

MOVING MICROPHONE

The microphone is moved from person to person around a small group or a circle when all are anxious to speak on an issue. A time limit can be set for each speaker.

CONVERSATION BALL

Draw a funny face on a tennis ball. When children want to speak they raise their hands and the ball is passed to them.

TAKING TURNS

Partners are assigned A or B. Then select an observer C. Any topic can be discussed. After a short discussion of 3–5 minutes C reports on how people took turns. A tally of turns taken can be kept and then reported on.

TOKEN A TURN

Some teachers hand out five or so tokens to each member of a pair. Children place a single token in the centre of the pair or group after they have spoken. This helps children share turns and makes very vocal children more aware of encouraging others to speak. Once someone has used all their tokens they must listen and not speak.

This activity needs to be carefully monitored so that quiet children don't feel they are being made to speak when they have little to say.

ATTENTIVE LISTENING

The skill of attentive listening is crucial to communication and co-operation. Being a good listener takes practice. Too often what appears to be listening is the listener silently rehearsing what he or she will say next and not listening to a partner at all. Being an attentive listener depends on the use of certain skills.*

The skill of *attending* requires:
1. Looking involved.
2. Getting involved.
3. Good eye contact.
4. A non-distracting environment.

Using these shows the speaker that you are interested, concerned and available for listening. Body language tells the speaker that you are involved. If you don't make eye contact and fold your arms and look away the message to the speaker is that you are not listening.

The skill of *following* requires:
1. Occasional prompting of the talker, for example:
   'Would you like to talk more about that?'

2. Some encouragement, such as head nods and expressions like 'I see', 'go on', 'yes'.
3. Asking limited questions.
4. An attentive silence.

Following the speaker involves some non-verbal communication and minimal intervention to enable the speaker to finish. It is difficult to avoid the temptation to take the agenda away from the speaker by asking questions that may be off the track.

The skill of *reflecting* requires:

1. Occasional paraphrasing of what the other person says.
2. Reflecting the other person's feelings.
3. Reflecting the other person's meanings.
4. Summarising what has been said from time to time.

Employing these skills demonstrates to the speaker that you are actively processing what is being said.

ACTIVITIES FOR ATTENTIVE LISTENING*

1. Students work in pairs: one is A and the other is B. A talks to B for a minute on a specific topic such as 'The food I like best.' B listens and talks to A for one minute about the same topic. A listens.
2. Students find another partner and nominate A and B.
   A talks to B for 1 minute.⎤ Same topic as before but not mentioning anything
   B talks to A for 1 minute.⎦ said last time
3. Students return to their first partner as in 1.
   A becomes B, recounting what B said.⎤ Using the first
   B becomes A, recounting what A said.⎦ person form
4. The whole group comes together to give feedback on their experiences in activities 1–3.
5. Students find a new partner and this time listen with eyes closed.
   A talks to B for 1 minute.⎤ New topic
   B talks to A for 1 minute.⎦
6. Same pairs as in 5 but this time students sit side by side and look directly in front. There is no eye contact.
   A talks to B for 1 minute.⎤ New topic
   B talks to A for 1 minute.⎦
   An observer can be used to note what happens in the sessions for 5 and 6.
7. The whole group discusses what happened when they listened.
8. The students then receive a checklist to remind them what twelve skills are necessary for careful listening (see next page). (Alternatively they could have these listed on a chart.)

*Activities for attentive listening adapted from ideas by Whitaker (1984).

Attentive listening checklist

Attending

1. Looking involved.
2. Getting involved.
3. Good eye contact.
4. A non-distracting environment.

Following

1. Occasional prompting of the talker: 'Would you like to talk more about that?'
2. Some encouragement: head nods and 'I see', 'go on', 'yes'.
3. Asking limited questions.
4. Attentive silence.

Reflecting

1. Occasional paraphrasing of what the other person said.
2. Reflecting the other person's feelings.
3. Reflecting the other person's meanings.
4. Summarising what has been said from time to time.

---

9. Students find a new partner. They practise the twelve skills needed for attentive listening.
   A talks to B for 3 minutes.⎤ New topic
   B talks to A for 3 minutes.⎦

10. Next pairs are observed as they discuss a new topic assigned by the group. A talks to B for three minutes. Topic of A's choice. C observes B using the checklist for active listening. C reports back on B's active listening. Students change roles and repeat the procedure so that each person is listener, talker, observer in turn.

11. Discuss as a whole group:
    • the importance of listening in communication
    • how we can improve as listeners.

MORE PARTNER ACTIVITIES

BACK TO BACK

Children sitting back to back each have a piece of paper and a pencil. Person A tells person B what to draw and draws exactly what the instructions describe on his or her own piece of paper. After five minutes the drawings are compared. Then person B gives person A drawing instructions.

MOUSE MAZE

Draw a maze with a mouse starting out to walk through a maze. In the centre of the maze draw some cheese. Make copies of the maze for each member of the pair. One person in each pair has a picture of the

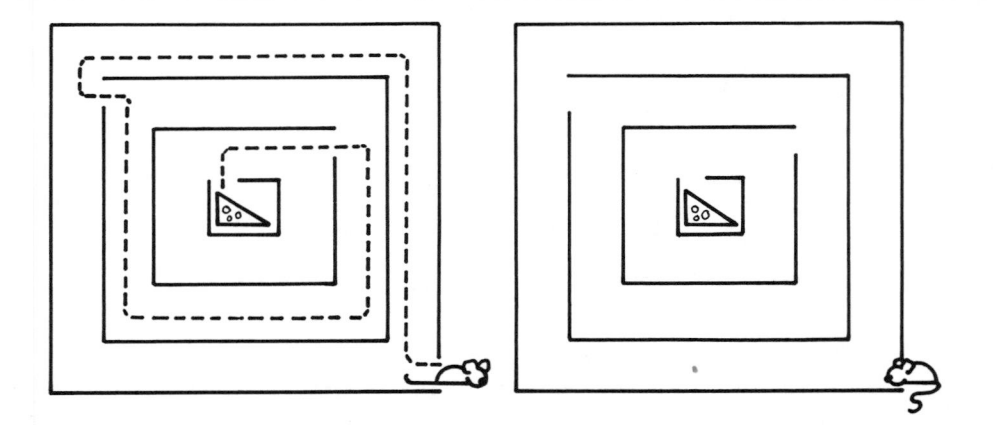

maze with the path the mouse took marked in. This person gives instructions on how to solve the puzzle. When the activity is finished compare each piece of paper.

A variation of this is to create a real maze in the classroom. Blindfold a 'mouse'. Give directions for the mouse to find the cheese. Some 'mice' will need someone to hold their hand to make sure they keep their balance.

TACKLING A STATEMENT

Cards, sticky labels or specially made badges with the following clearly written on the front are needed.

++ = strongly agree	-· = disagree
+ = agree	-- = strongly disagree

? = can't decide or don't know

A controversial statement such as 'TV should be banned during the week' or 'Boys only should be allowed to play cricket' is written on the blackboard. Students are asked to reflect upon the statements for 2 minutes and then choose and wear a badge that best represents their response to the statement.

They next discuss the statement with a person wearing the same badge (3 minutes). Students then move on to discuss the statement with a person wearing a badge one position removed from their own badge (3 minutes). Then students talk with people two or three positions away from their own (3 minutes). Finally students return to their original partner and share ideas they have heard. Remind students at each change that active listening is to be encouraged.

QUICK CHATS

Partners take turns to describe the best thing that has ever happened, or the worst, or the most embarrassing event. After A recounts the story and B has listened actively the roles are switched. After each story has been told the pairs return to the group and A tells B's story in the first person so the story sounds as though it really happened to A. Then B tells A's story in a similar way. This activity is a good one for increasing empathy for others of different gender, race or ability.

GOSSIP

In this version of gossip the class is divided into groups with eight members. Four members of each group are then sent outside and are called in one at a time. The first to come in is told a message like these:

> To get to the library you go up the stairs then turn right. Walk through the next door on your left. Turn right and you are there.

> Last week you left your lunch at home and your mother rang the school to remind you to leave early so you could go home to collect it. Frank was meant to give you the message. I think he was playing football so he probably forgot. Perhaps he told someone else to tell you. Next time I'll ask Tim to give you the message.

This person repeats the message to the next person and so on until all four are back with the group. Chances are that the message will change from person to person and by the time the fourth person hears the message it will be quite different. The observers then discuss how the message has changed.

CONCENTRIC CIRCLES

Divide the class into two groups. One group makes an inner circle and the others form a circle around this group. The people in the outer circle watch as the inner circle breaks up into pairs and discusses any topic of general interest to the class. The outer circle watches for active listening behaviour. After 5–10 minutes stop the conversation and the observers report to the class on positive listening behaviours. Alternatively the observers can report directly to the person or pair they were watching.

Some topics: 'What rules are really important in the classroom?'

'What is your idea of a perfect teacher or parent?'

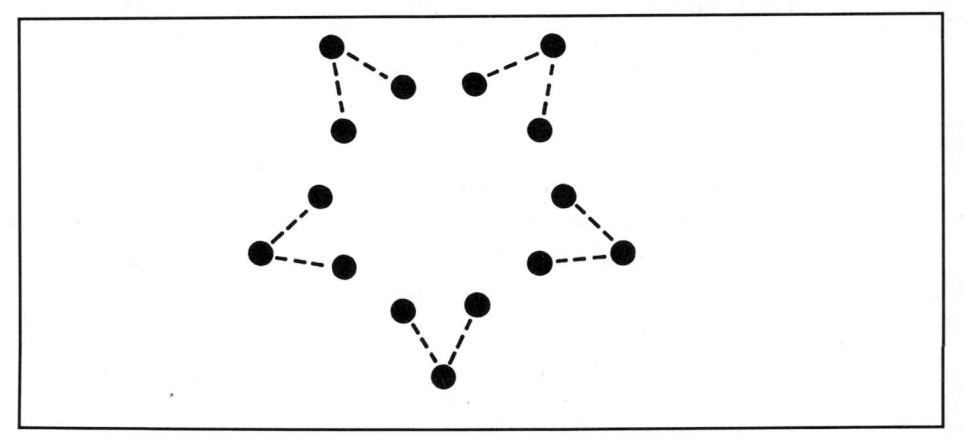

MOVING CIRCLES

This is a variation on concentric circles. Children form an outer circle and an inner circle. They face each other to make pairs.

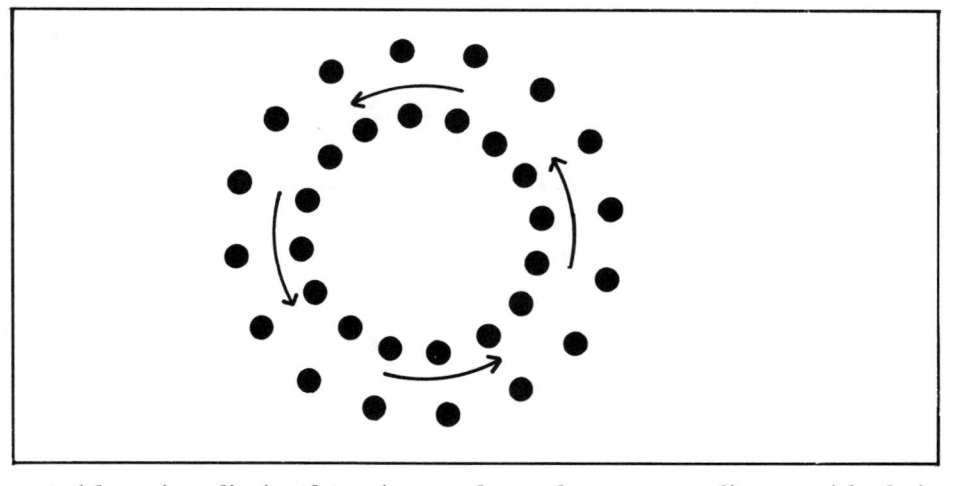

With a time limit of 2 minutes they take turns to discuss with their partner issues such as 'Schools should be held from 9–12 each day of the week' or 'Junk food should be banned'. When the time is up the outer circle people move on to the next person to their right. Taking turns is essential.

This is a good way to hear a range of ideas or to air solutions to a difficult problem. Another way to do this is to have the inner circle argue for an issue. The outer circle argues against an issue.

RADIO INTERVIEWS

In pairs children take it in turns to interview each other for a radio show. Before actually making the tape recording children rehearse these questions and the answers they will give.

- What was your first day of school like?
- Who was/is your favourite group of friends?
- Where did you go on your first holiday?
- What is your most vivid childhood memory?

The children can play back the tape and listen as they each play interviewer and interviewee.

PROBABILITIES

Change is something we can be sure will happen. Children in pairs write down the following:

- Three things that will definitely happen
- Three things that will definitely not happen
- Three things that will probably happen
- Three things that will probably not happen
- Three things that might possibly happen.

Now they explain their predictions to another pair.

REACTIONS

Form groups of six. After hearing a guest speaker or watching a video children are given 15 minutes or so to write (or draw) three reactions to the event on small cards. The reactions are their true feelings about the event and can be a single word or a paragraph. Then the reactions are put into the centre of the group. People take turns to look at the cards and select three cards (not their own) that match or are close to their own opinion. Now the children form pairs and tell their partner what the cards they are holding indicate. They next try to work out a joint view or summary of a few sentences with their partner. Then they report their pair's view to the whole class. This activity works well if children have viewed a controversial film or video and a range of opinions have been generated.

TIMELINES

In pairs use one piece of paper and two different marker pens. Ask the children to draw individual timelines with key events in their lives noted on the timeline. When the timeline is complete find similarities and differences between their lives.

A variation of this is to ask pairs to do a future timeline from the present day into the future. Again discuss the similarities.

CO-OPERATIVE SHAPES

This is a classic activity for co-operation. Have children in groups of four with one of the group as observer. Give the other members of the group one envelope with cardboard cut into various shapes. Put all the pieces of cardboard numbered A into an A envelope and B into a B envelope (see diagram on next page).

Rules

1. There is no verbal communication between people. There are no non-verbal winks, nods or signals.
2. All pieces not needed by a person are placed in the centre of the table. Pieces are not passed directly from hand to hand between people.
3. People can decline to take part at any time.

The observer watches for co-operation and reports on the positive examples. All participants will want to discuss frustration with those who finish quickly yet have a piece needed by another.

Variations

Use circles or build up the number of participants to five. Use shapes where there are several possibilities for creating shapes.

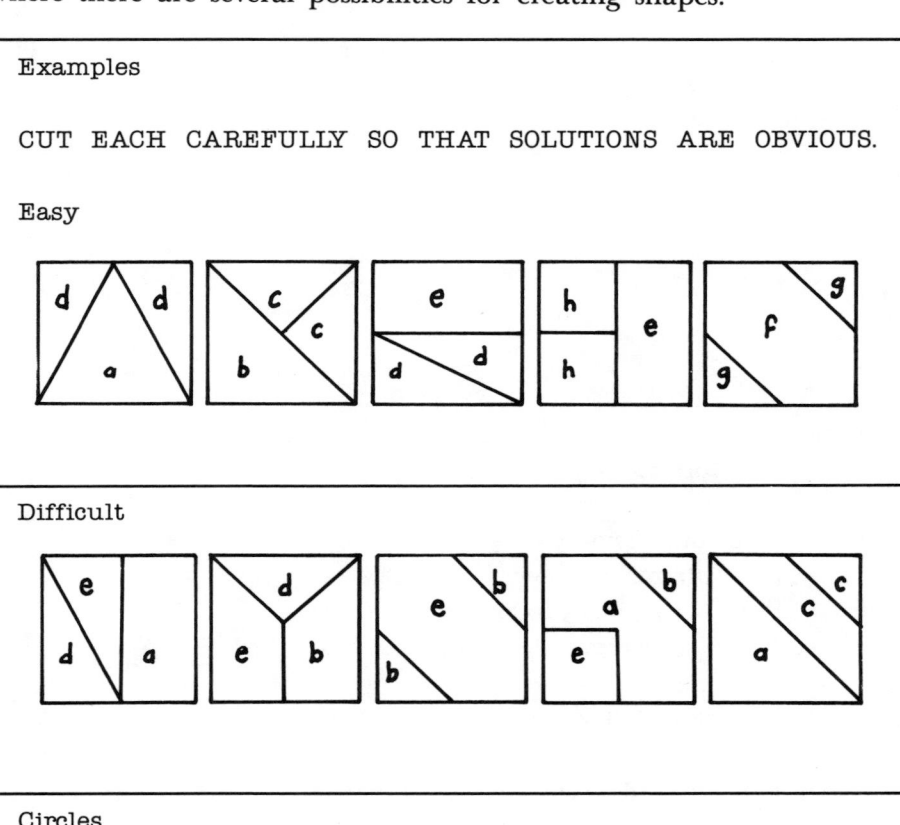

Examples

CUT EACH CAREFULLY SO THAT SOLUTIONS ARE OBVIOUS.

Easy

Difficult

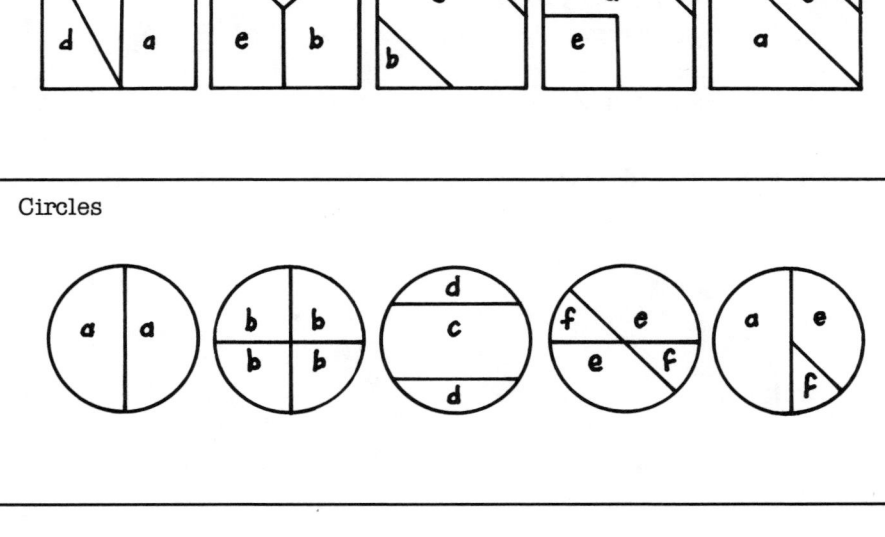

Circles

CARDS

The following activities can be put on cards for partner activities for young children.

Collage

With a partner

1. Find magazines, paste and scissors.
2. Look through the magazine and find pictures that you like.
3. Paste the pictures that you both like on one piece of paper.
4. Tell each other why you both like the pictures.

What to buy

With a partner

1. Take two catalogues from two discount stores.
2. With your partner agree on five things you would both like to buy.
3. Find five things you both wouldn't like to buy.
4. Record on the piece of paper the five things you would buy and five you wouldn't buy.

Would buy	Wouldn't buy

Friends

With a partner

1. Find an egg timer.
2. Each take a piece of paper and a pencil.
3. Turn the egg timer over.
4. Write words to describe your partner.
5. When the timer runs out write words to describe two other people in the class.

Newspaper reporter

With a partner

1. Take turns to be a newspaper reporter and ask each other questions.
2. Take three question cards from the envelope.
3. Ask your partner these questions.
4. Then your partner takes three questions.
5. Continue on until all questions have been asked.

Questions

- If you had three wishes what would they be?
- What makes you happy?
- What makes you sad?
- What is your favourite time of day?
- What needs to be changed at school?
- What do you do on the weekends?
- What do you like to do on the weekends?
- What films do you like?
- What is your favourite food?
- What does your house look like?
- What do you like about your home?
- What makes you angry?
- What makes a good friend?

LANGUAGE ARTS

PARTNER READING
This can be organised in many ways.

1. A can read aloud and B can listen and ask a question of A. Then the roles are changed for the next page or segment. Children can agree to be reader or listener for a longer extract. The listener asks the reader critical or creative questions after the piece has been read. These ideas work with young children who like to reassure themselves that they are reading by reading out loud.

2. For more proficient readers who read silently partners may read, then summarise alternative paragraphs if the text is dense or alternative pages if the text is easy.

3. Alternatively readers may set questions jointly before they read, then read to find the answers. The answers can be discussed and debated after the piece has been read.

4. An individual reader A sets questions after reading a novel. When another child B has read the book and set questions the two readers discuss the questions set by A. They then discuss the questions set

by B. For example if a child has read *Space Demons*, a series of questions like the following could be set for a partner conference.

- How did Mario help the children?
- How would you solve the problem if it happened to you?
- Are computer freaks living in a different world?
- What would happen if...?

Children record the date and title of the book on a chart. An alternative idea is to have one question card set by the first reader and this card stays in the book. All future readers of the book from then on form pairs and discuss the questions.

PARTNER WRITING

This can occur at several stages of the writing process.*

Planning Stage

1. Two people discuss the ideas and one person writes.
2. Two people share research information on a topic, say spiders, and one writes or both could write separate reports.
3. One person does the research and the other writes up the report with the researcher offering suggestions.

Drafting Stage

1. Several writers divide the work into sections and each writes one part.
2. Co-authors work together sharing the drafting and the pencil.
3. One writer combines the writing of several others into one larger piece of narrative or informational text.

Revising Stage

1. One person edits and reorganises the draft of another person.
2. One person adapts the work of another, for example modifying a piece for a younger audience.
3. Once person puts together the chunks written by several others.

In working together with writing ask questions and respond in supportive ways, e.g.:

- What characters were vivid?
- Describe an experience that you have had that is similar.
- Describe which section of the piece was the most vivid. Why was this so?
- What thoughts did you have as a reader?
  Suggestions for accepting feedback are:
- Don't quarrel with someone else's reaction.
- Be quiet and listen.

*Based in part on Fleming (1988).

PARTNER SPELLING

Children help each other learn personal spelling words or for a topic. If these words are tested the partners receive an average score of both children's total. A shared score encourages both to use the most effective strategy for remembering the spelling. Careful observation is needed to make sure that a range of strategies is used. And of course, careful pairing of students is necessary.

Some words can be sounded phonetically, some can only be learned visually and others can be learned through the morphographic pattern or structure.

◆

APPENDIX 3:

CO-OPERATION IN

PICTURE BOOKS

◆

Albert, Burton. *Mine, Yours, Ours.* A. Whitman, Chicago, 1977.

Alexandra, Martha, G. *I'll Be the Horse If You'll Play with Me.* Dial Press, New York, 1975.

Aliki. *We Are Best Friends.* Piccolo, London, 1984.

Barkin, Carol & James, Elizabeth. *Sometimes I Hate School.* Raintree Pubs. Ltd, Milwaukee, 1975.

_____. *Doing Things Together.* Raintree Pubs Ltd, Milwaukee, 1975.

Beim, Lorraine & Beim, Jerrold. *Two Is a Team.* Harcourt Brace Jovanovich, New York, 1974.

Berry, Joy Wilt. *Fighting.* Grolier, Danbury, CT, 1982.

Blaine, Marge. *The Terrible Thing that Happened at our House.* Puffin, Harmondsworth, 1976.

Bonsall, Crosby Newell. *Who's a Pest?* World's Work, 1978.

Brandenberg, Franz & Aliki. *The Hit of the Party.* Piccolo, London, 1985.

_____ . *Nice New Neighbours.* Hamish Hamilton, London, 1979.

Browne, Anthony. *Piggybook.* Julia MacRae, London, 1986.

Burningham, John. *Mr Gumpy's Outing.* Cape, London, 1970.

Coleridge, Ann & Harvey, Roland. *The Friends of Emily Culpepper.* Five Mile Press, Melbourne, 1983.

Corey, Dorothy. *Everybody Takes Turns, We All Share.* A. Whitman, Chicago, 1980.

Croll, Carolyn. *Too Many Babas.* Harper & Row, New York, 1979.

Croser, Josephine & McLean-Carr, Carol. *Crunch the Crocodile.* Ashton, Gosford, 1986.

Emberley, Barbara & Emberley, Ed. *Drummer Hoff*. Bodley Head, London, 1970.

Fox, Mem & Ellis, Lorraine. *Feathers & Fools*. Ashwood House, Melbourne, 1989.

Heine, Helme. *Friends*. Collins Picture Lions, London, 1984.

_____ . *The Most Wonderful Egg in the World*. Collins Picture Lions, London, 1985.

Hoban, Russell. *Harvey's Hideout*. Puffin, Harmondsworth, 1976.

_____ . *The Sorely Trying Day*. Harper & Row, New York, 1964.

_____ . *Tom and the Two Handles*. World's Work, 1977.

Hughes, Shirley. *Alfie Gets in First*. Collins Picture Lions, London, 1982.

_____ . *Alfie Gives a Hand*. Collins Picture Lions, London, 1985.

_____ . *Dogger*. Bodley Head, London, 1977.

_____ . *Helpers*. Collins Picture Lions, London, 1978.

Hutchins, Pat. *The Best Train Set Ever*. Bodley Head, London, 1979.

Keats, Ezra Jack. *Peter's Chair*. Bodley Head, London, 1986.

Kerr, Judith. *Mog, the Forgetful Cat*. Collins, 1986.

Klein, Norma. *Visiting Pamela*. Dial, New York, 1979.

Lionni, Leo. *Swimmy*. Pantheon, Westminister, MD, 1963.

McKee, David. *Tusk, Tusk*. Collins, London, 1978.

Minarik, Else Holmelund. *No Fighting, No Biting!* World's Work, 1969.

Ormerod, Jan. *101 Things to Do with a Baby*. Kestrel, Harmondsworth, 1984.

Sharmat, Marjorie. *I'm not Oscar's Friend Anymore*. Dutton, New York, 1975.

_____ . *Sometimes Mama and Papa Fight!* Harper & Row, New York, 1980.

_____ . *The Trip*. Macmillan, New York, 1976.

Sherman, Ivan. *I Do Not Like It when my Friend Comes to Visit*. Harcourt, Brace, Jovanovich, New York, 1973.

Steadman, Ralph. *The Bridge*. Collins, 1975.

Steig, William. *Amos and Boris*. Farrar, Straus & Giroux, New York, 1971.

Udry, Janice May. *Let's Be Enemies*. Harper & Row, New York, 1961.

Vigna, Judith. *The Hiding House*. A. Whitman, Chicago, 1979.

Vincent, Gabrielle. *Bravo, Ernest and Celestine*. Collins Picture Lions, London, 1983.

_____ . *Ernest and Celestine*. Collins Picture Lions, London, 1983.

Waber, Bernard. *Bernard*. Houghton Mifflin, Boston, 1982.

Wagner, Jenny & Brooks, Ron. *John Brown, Rose and the Midnight Cat*. Penguin, Melbourne, 1986.

Wildsmith, Brian. *The Hunter and his Dog*. Oxford University Press, 1984.

_____ . *The Lion and the Rat*. Oxford University Press, 1986.

Zolotow, Charlotte. *The New Friend*. Abelard, New York, 1968.

_____ . *The Quarreling Book*. Harper & Row, New York, 1963.

_____ . *The Unfriendly Book*. Harper & Row, New York, 1975.

◆

APPENDIX 4:

CO-OPERATION IN BOOKS FOR MID AND UPPER PRIMARY

◆

Alexandra, Lloyd. *The Prydain Chronicles*. Heinemann, London, 1966–1979.

Bawden, Nina. *A Handful of Thieves*. Gollancz, London, 1967.

Boston, Lucy. *A Stranger at Greene Knowe*. Faber & Faber, London, 1961.

Brown, Fern. *You're Somebody Special on a Horse*. A. Whitman, Chicago, 1977.

Byars, Betsy. *The Eighteenth Emergency*. Bodley Head, London, 1974.

_____ . *The Pinballs*. Bodley Head, London, 1977.

Chambers, Aidan. *The Present Takers*. Bodley Head, London, 1983.

Cleaver, Vera & Cleaver, Bill. *Dust of the Earth*. Lippincott Junior Books, New York, 1975.

Clifford, Ethel. *The Rocking Chair Rebellion*. Houghton Mifflin, Boston, 1978.

De Trevino, E. *I, Juan de Pareja*. Farrar, Straus & Giroux, New York, 1965.

French, Simon, *Cannily, Cannily*. Angus & Robertson, Sydney, 1981.

Godden, Rumer. *Mr McFadden's Halloween*. Viking, New York, 1975.

Hoban, Russell. *A Mouse and His Child*. Harper & Row, New York, 1967.

Kastner, Erich. *Emil and the Detectives*. Cape, London, 1959.

Kelleher, Victor. *Taronga*. Penguin, Melbourne, 1986.

Klein, Robin. *Boss of the Pool*. Omnibus, Adelaide, 1986.

Lawrence, Louise, *Children of the Dust*. Harper & Row, New York, 1985.

Lewis, C. S. *The Narnia Chronicles*. Collins, London, various dates.

Long, Judy. *Volunteer Spring*. Archway, 1977.

Mattingley, Christobel. *The Angel with a Mouth Organ*. Hodder & Stoughton, Sydney, 1984.

Mazer, Harry. *The War on Villa Street*. Dell, New York, n.d.

Melton, David. *A Boy Called Hopeless*. Independence Press, Independence, MO, 1976.

Needle, Jan. *My Mate Shofiq*. Collins, London, 1978.

Park, Ruth. *Callie's Castle*. Angus & Robertson, Sydney, 1985.

_____ . *Callie's Family*. Angus & Robertson. Sydney, 1988.

Renner, Beverley Hollett. *The Hideaway Summer*. Harper & Row, New York, 1978.

Rubinstein, Gillian. *Space Demons*. Omnibus, Adelaide, 1986.

_____ . *Answers to Brut*. Omnibus, Adelaide, 1988.

_____ . *Skymaze*. Penguin, Melbourne, 1989.

Tobias, Tobi. *The Quitting Deal*. Puffin, Harmondsworth, 1979.

REFERENCES & FURTHER READING

Burton, C.B., 1987, 'Problems in children's peer relationships: a broadening perspective' in Katz, L.G. (ed), *Current Topics in Early Childhood Education*, vol. 7, Ablex, Norwood, NJ.

Cooper, L.; Johnson, D.W.; Johnson, R.T. & Wilderson, F. 1980, 'The effects of co-operation, competition and individualization on cross-ethnic, cross-sex, and cross-ability friendships', *Journal of Social Psychology*, vol. 111, pp. 243–52.

Doise, Willem & Mugny, Gabriel 1984, *The Social Development of the Individual*, Pergamon Press, New York.

Fleming, Margaret 1988, 'Getting out of the vacuum', in *Focus on Collaborative Learning*, NCTE.

Glasser, William 1969, *Schools Without Failure*, Harper & Row, New York.

_____ 1986, *Control Theory in the Classroom*, Harper & Row, New York.

Haggard, Martha 1985, 'An interactive strategies approach to content area reading', *Journal of Reading*, vol. 29, Dec.

Hill, Timothy and Reed, Kaarin 1989, 'Promoting social competence at preschool: the implications of a co-operative games program', *Australian Journal of Early Childhood*, vol. 14., no. 4, pp. 11–16.

Johnson, David W. & Johnson, Roger T. 1975, *Joining Together: Group Theory and Group Skills*, Prentice Hall, Englewood Cliffs, NJ.

_____ 1981, 'Effects of co-operation and individual learning experiences on interethnic interaction', *Journal of Educational Psychology*, vol. 73, pp. 454–9.

_____ 1983, 'The socialisation and achievement crisis — are co-operative learning experiences the solution?' in Bickman, L. (ed), *Applied Social Psychology Annual 4*, Sage Publications, Beverly Hills, CA.

_____ 1985, *Warm-ups, Grouping Strategies and Group Activities*, Interaction Book, Co., Edina, MN.

_____ 1987, *Cooperation and Competition*, Lawrence Eribaum, Hillsdale, NJ.

_____ various dates, *Our Link*, Co-operative Learning Center, 202 Pattee Hall, 150 Pillsbury Drive, Minneapolis, MN.

_____ & Holubec, Edythe Johnson 1986, *Circles of Learning: Co-operation in the Classroom*, Interaction Book Co., Edina, MN.

_____ 1987, *Structuring Co-operative Learning*, Interaction Book Co., Edina, MN.

Johnson, David W.; Maruyama, G.; Johnson, Roger T.; Nelson, D. & Skon, L. 1981, 'Effects of co-operative, competitive and individualistic goal structures on achievement: a meta-analysis', *Psychological Bulletin*, vol. 89, pp. 47–62.

Lewin, K. 1948, *Resolving Social Conflicts*, Harper & Row, New York, 1948.

Meek, Margaret 1982, *Learning to Read*, Bodley Head, London.

Norem-Hebeisen, A. & Johnson, D.W. 1981, 'Relationships between co-operative, competitive and individualistic attitudes and differential aspects of self-esteem', *Journal of Personality*, vol. 49, pp. 415–25.

Pike, Graham & Selby, David 1988, *Global Teacher, Global Learner*, Hodder & Stoughton, London, 1988.

Rosenblatt, Louise 1978, *Literature as Exploration*, Noble & Noble, New York.

Sapon-Shevin, Mara, 'Teaching co-operation' in Cartledge, Gwendolyn & Milburn, Joanne Fellows (eds) 1986, *Teaching Social Skills to Children*, Pergamon Press, New York.

Slavin, Robert; Schlomo, Sharon; Kagan, Spencer; Lazarowitz, Webb Clark & Schmuck, Richard 1985, *Learning to Co-operate, Co-operating to Learn*, Plenum Press, New York.

Smith, Frank 1978, *Understanding Reading*, 2nd ed., Holt, Rinehart & Winston, New York.

Spivak, G. & Shure, M. B. 1974, *Social Adjustment of Young Children: A Cognitive Approach to Solving Real-life Problems*, Jossey Bass, San Francisco.

Yager, S; Johnson, R.T.; Johnson, D.W. & Snider, B. 1975, 'The effects of co-operative and individualistic experiences on positive and negative cross-handicap relationships', *Contemporary Educational Psychology*, vol. 10, no. 2, April, pp. 127–38.

Whitaker, Patrick 1984, 'Learning process', *World Studies Journal*, vol. 5, no. 2.

Balson, Maurice. *Understanding Classroom Behaviour.* Australian Council for Educational Research, Hawthorn, 1987.

Crary, Elizabeth. *Kids Can Co-operate.* Parker Bros, 1984.

Dalton, Joan. *Adventures in Thinking.* Nelson, Melbourne, 1988.

Golub, Jeff & the Committee on Classroom Practices, NCTE. *Focus on Collaborative Learning.* NCTE, Urbana, IL, 1988.

Johnson, David. *Reaching Out.* Prentice Hall, Englewood Cliffs, NJ, 1972.

Kamii, Constance & De Vries, Rheta. *Group Games in Early Education.* National Association for the Education of Young Children, Washington, DC, 1980.

Orlick, Terry. *The Second Co-operative Sports & Games Book.* Pantheon, New York, 1982.

Observation Sheet

Co-operative skill	Name	Name	Name
Encouraging			

This page may be photocopied free of copyright.

Individual checklist of how I co-operated

Name _____

	No	Sometimes	Yes

I helped
our group by: _____

Adding ideas _____

Encouraging
others _____

Summarising _____

Clarifying
 ideas _____

Something I'll work on next time is

_____

_____

_____

_____

Date _____

My achievements	My goals

This page may be photocopied free of copyright.

Observation Sheet

Ideas contributed _____

_____

_____

_____

Encouraged _____

_____

_____

Summarised ideas _____

_____

_____

Clarified ideas _____

_____

_____